WRITING **ABOUT** ARCHITECTURE

Architecture Briefs is a Princeton Architectural Press series that addresses a variety of single topics of interest to architecture students and professionals. Field-specific and technical information, ranging from hand-drawn to digital methods, are presented in a user-friendly manner alongside basics of architectural thought, design, and construction. The series familiarizes readers with the concepts and skills necessary to successfully translate ideas into built form.

ALSO IN THE ARCHITECTURE BRIEF SERIES:

ARCHITECTS DRAW
SUE FERGUSON GUSSOW
ISBN 978-1-56898-740-8

ARCHITECTURAL LIGHTING:
DESIGNING WITH LIGHT AND SPACE
HERVE DESCOTTES, CECILIA E. RAMOS
ISBN 978-1-56898-938-9

ARCHITECTURAL PHOTOGRAPHY THE
DIGITAL WAY
GERRY KOPELOW
ISBN 978-1-56898-697-5

BUILDING ENVELOPES: AN INTEGRATED
APPROACH
JENNY LOVELL
ISBN 978-1-56898-818-4

DIGITAL FABRICATIONS: ARCHITECTURAL
AND MATERIAL TECHNIQUES
LISA IWAMOTO
ISBN 978-1-56898-790-3

ETHICS FOR ARCHITECTS: 50 DILEMMAS
OF PROFESSIONAL PRACTICE
THOMAS FISHER
ISBN 978-1-56898-946-4

MATERIAL STRATEGIES: INNOVATIVE
APPLICATIONS IN ARCHITECTURE
BLAINE BROWNELL
ISBN 978-1-56898-986-0

MODEL MAKING
MEGAN WERNER
ISBN 978-1-56898-870-2

OLD BUILDING, NEW DESIGN:
ARCHITECTURAL
TRANSFORMATIONS
CHARLES BLOSZIES
ISBN 978-1-61689-035-3

PHILOSOPHY FOR ARCHITECTS
BRANKO MITROVIĆ
ISBN 978-1-56898-994-5

WRITING
ABOUT
ARCHITECTURE

MASTERING THE LANGUAGE OF BUILDINGS AND CITIES

Alexandra Lange

With photographs by Jeremy M. Lange

PRINCETON ARCHITECTURAL PRESS, NEW YORK

PUBLISHED BY
PRINCETON ARCHITECTURAL PRESS
37 EAST SEVENTH STREET
NEW YORK, NEW YORK 10003

FOR A FREE CATALOG OF BOOKS, CALL
1-800-722-6657. VISIT OUR WEBSITE AT
WWW.PAPRESS.COM.

EDITOR: LINDA LEE
DESIGNER: DEB WOOD

SPECIAL THANKS TO: BREE ANNE
APPERLEY, SARA BADER, NICK BEATTY,
NICOLA BEDNAREK BROWER, JANET
BEHNING, FANNIE BUSHIN, MEGAN
CAREY, CARINA CHA, RUSSELL
FERNANDEZ, JAN HAUX, DIANE
LEVINSON, JENNIFER LIPPERT, GINA
MORROW, JOHN MYERS, KATHARINE
MYERS, MARGARET ROGALSKI, DAN
SIMON, ANDREW STEPANIAN, PAUL
WAGNER, AND JOSEPH WESTON OF
PRINCETON ARCHITECTURAL PRESS
—KEVIN C. LIPPERT, PUBLISHER

LIBRARY OF CONGRESS CATALOGING-IN-
PUBLICATION DATA

LANGE, ALEXANDRA.
 WRITING ABOUT ARCHITECTURE :
 MASTERING THE LANGUAGE OF
BUILDINGS AND CITIES / ALEXANDRA
LANGE ; WITH PHOTOGRAPHS BY JEREMY
M. LANGE. — 1ST ED.
     P. CM. — (ARCHITECTURE BRIEF
SERIES)
 ISBN 978-1-61689-053-7 (PBK. : ALK.
PAPER)
1. ARCHITECTURAL CRITICISM. I.
LANGE, JEREMY M. II. TITLE. III.
TITLE: MASTERING THE LANGUAGE OF
BUILDINGS AND CITIES.
 NA2599.5.L36 2012
 720.1—DC23

                                        2011032750

How to Be an Architecture Critic

BUILDINGS ARE EVERYWHERE, large and small, ugly and beautiful, ambitious and dumb. We walk among them and live inside them but are largely passive dwellers in cities of towers, houses, open spaces, and shops we had no hand in creating. But we are their best audience. Owners, clients, and residents come and go, but architecture lives on, acting a role in the life of the city and its citizens long after the original players are gone. Architecture critics can praise and pick on new designs, but their readership has lately been too limited. We talk (in person, on blogs) about homes as investments, building sites as opportunities, unsold condominiums as an economic disaster, but all of that real-estate chatter sidesteps the physical reality of projects built and unbuilt. Rather than just talking about money, we should also be talking about height and bulk, style and sustainability, openness of architecture and of process. Design is not the icing on the cake but what makes architecture out of buildings and the places we want to live and eat and shop rather than avoid. Instead of less talk, what we need are more critics—citizen critics— equipped with the desire and the vocabulary to remake the city.

There are times when city dwellers have been roused from passivity. Disaster (Ground Zero) and personal affront (NIMBYism) make protestors out of us all, but we are rarely roused by the day-to-day, brick-by-brick additions that have the most power to change our environment. We know what we already like but not how to describe it, or how to change it, or how to change our minds. We need to learn how to read a building, an urban plan, and a developer's rendering, and to see where critique might make a difference.

This is a handbook that demonstrates how critics look at those buildings, parks, and plans, and shows how anyone can follow in the footsteps of those writers. It is based on courses in architecture criticism I teach at New York University and the School of Visual Arts—classes that simultaneously offer a foundational history of twentieth-century criticism and lessons in doing it yourself.

In the courses and in this book, I connect the reader and the writer, the citizen and the critic, in two ways. First and foremost by reading and comparing exemplary pieces of critical writing. Each chapter in this book is preceded by a complete essay or lengthy excerpt from a piece of critical writing about a different building or urban type: Lewis Mumford on skyscrapers, Herbert Muschamp on museums, Michael Sorkin on preservation, Charles W. Moore on the monument, Frederick Law Olmsted on parks, Jane Jacobs on cities. In the text that follows the essay, there is a close reading of that essay, discussing the specific questions raised by the critic about the type and the methods he or she uses to raise those questions.

There is no one right way to write architecture criticism, but the critics discussed in this book all get it right in different ways. An understanding of their style, editorial judgment, and mode of argument can help future critics to get it right as well. Digging into Olmsted's principles of park design, for example, one gains a sense of the history the landscape architect is working against or within. Reading Karrie Jacobs's review of the far more recent High Line, one sees those principles considered and rejected in the contemporary park. There is continuity between Central Park and the High Line, but it takes a deeper knowledge of American park design to see it.

After reading the original text and the accompanying discussion, the critic should have the tools to discuss the building type and be able to choose the history, method, and elements that seem most relevant. The critical essay is typically brief (in a newspaper, approximately twelve hundred words), so one must limit the questions asked and answered. Quotations from others discussing the same type or even the same building illustrate the vast array of possible *themes* available to a critic. The theme is the narrative line in any piece of criticism, an idea about the architecture or architect introduced at the beginning of the essay, bolstered by evidence in the body of the text, and returned to at the end. It gives a critique shape and allows the critic to impose his or her personality on the project in question. (The italicized terms are ones to which I will return in the text—key considerations for any piece of critical writing.)

Three critics, standing side-by-side, looking at the same wall, can have completely different things to say about that wall without ever disagreeing. One might consider the wall's material, comparing it to other structures that use marble, glass, or metal in similar ways. The other might ignore its physical aspect and discuss instead how it separates building from street, circulation from offices, public from private. Yet another might imagine the wall as a backdrop for interpersonal drama. In teaching it is often hard for me to repress my own opinions about a building or plan, but I try always to make it clear: there is no right answer about whether a building is good or bad, beautiful or ugly, accessible or imposing. The critic needs to define terms, choose a theme, then evaluate the architecture within those guidelines. Knowing something about the larger critical history of the type will be essential to choosing appropriate parameters.

Another way critics define their agenda is by selecting an *approach*. By the end of the book, the reader will have been exposed to four major critical approaches of the latter half of the twentieth century. I list them here but will discuss them in more detail in the chapters. The first is the formal approach. *Formal*, in art historical terminology, does not mean damask napkins and silver but a primary emphasis on the visual—the building or object's form. Both Huxtable and Mumford come to their judgments through intense looking. They write about what they see from the street—the building's organization, materials, connections. They literally walk you through the building, describing and picking at it as they go, suggesting improvements. This approach offers one of the easiest methods of *organization*: the walk-through, as exemplified by Mumford's tour of Lever House, examined in chapter 1. Organization is the structure of the review: Is it a three-part argument? A stroll in the park? A visual analysis from steps to spire? Because we are writing about a visual art, there is often a parallel between the literary and the architectonic organization.

The second approach is experiential, as created and defined by Muschamp, the late *New York Times* critic. Muschamp is also descriptive in his writing, but he expresses the way a building makes him (and by extension, the reader) feel. His reviews can start anywhere in a building, even at the airport of the city in which the building stands (as in his review of the Guggenheim Bilbao, discussed in chapter 2), and often mix in other media—movies, art, books, poetry—in order to make the emotional connection between architecture and reader.

The third approach is historical, which is primarily identifiable in the work of the present-day *New Yorker* architecture critic Paul Goldberger. He is interested in the architect's career and in fitting buildings within that (limited) framework. A Goldberger review may be as much about personality and presence on the world stage as it is about a building, but it also offers a sense of context missing from other critics' work. One is left with a sense of completeness, of having a thorough survey.

The final critical approach, seen in the criticism of Sorkin (chapter 3) and more broadly in the career of Jacobs (chapter 6) is that of the activist. Their first questions are not visual or experiential: Who loses? Who wins? These critics feel that they are the defenders of the city and of the people, and analyze projects primarily for economic and social benefits. Sorkin, in particular, knows the value of a good *kicker*: a last line that makes you laugh, however sourly.

These approaches are, like themes, only starting points. As the internet opens up more avenues for criticism, the pie may be sliced more thinly, generating a sustainable critic, an accessibility critic, and a feminist critic of architecture. Some have found the formal approach wanting in the late twentieth and early twenty-first centuries, feeling that it can remove buildings from their cities and place too much emphasis on materials and appearances above their role in the urban landscape. I disagree—at least as the approach is practiced by Huxtable and Mumford—but it is worth considering that some approaches may be played out.

In my courses, after reading and analyzing the work of critics, I lead my students on field trips to new buildings, parks, even information centers; the students all review the field-trip subject. They then read and critique each others' reviews in preparation for an in-class workshop. They are evaluated on the revision of their original review, written with my input as well as that of their classmates. It is in personally writing a piece of criticism where abstract lessons about theme, organization, and approach really take hold. And this aspect of the course is trickier to put in book form.

The course alternates between reading sessions, field trips, and writing workshops because the three activities create a feedback loop. Familiarity with exemplary models for criticism (the readings) is essential to be able to write good criticism but spending too much time in the classroom does not a critic make. At the end of each chapter is a checklist of questions meant to facilitate the kinds of conversations that occur during workshop sessions. The questions help guide the writer to be constructive in his or her criticism and also suggest directions that await exploration. What do we ask of our parks today that we did not in the past? How do skyscrapers operate as billboards in the digital age? How can blogs take up the mantle of Jacobs? Asking and answering these questions it is harder than it seems. That's why you have to go out and do it.

So how do you read a building? As with any craft, start with the best example you can think of and pick it apart until you see how it was done. The piece I return to has a title as applicable to the text as it is to the spaces the text describes: "Sometimes We Do It Right," written by Huxtable and published in the *New York Times* on March 31, 1968. Huxtable's review of Skidmore, Owings & Merrill's (SOM) 1967 Marine Midland Bank Building at 140 Broadway in Lower Manhattan describes the miraculous way architecture and public art of different eras can come together to create a great urban space.

      Huxtable reviews the office tower, but only in passing, since for 95 percent of New Yorkers, its importance will only ever be as a backdrop for Isamu Noguchi's *Red Cube* sculpture. She only skims the surfaces of all its neighbors, noting their varied materials, historical styles, and how their presence alters the streetscape. The sidewalks and open spaces are her main concern. Noguchi's cube claims the plaza that is Marine Midland's front yard, but there are views around the cube and through the downtown canyons that are equally striking. The contrast of solid and void is what makes this corner "right" and what makes any city right.

      What differentiates one corner, one neighborhood, or one city from another is the ratio of building to open space: the heights of Midtown versus the low brownstones of Brooklyn in New York or the peaks of central Lake Shore Drive versus the residential neighborhoods to the north and south in Chicago. As Huxtable writes, "Space is meaningless without scale, containment, boundaries and direction." Space needs as much shaping as the act of building, and in this review she balances the need for architecture and the need for open space, writing from the perspective of the pedestrian and adding a sense of history to the everyday experience of walking the streets.

      In a way, the structure of this book imitates her balance between solid and void. In the first three chapters the critics evaluate specific buildings. In the next three they look at the places around those buildings—monuments, parks and neighborhoods—an effort that requires less discussion of architectural style and more of the movements of people.

Few practitioners of criticism meant to be critics. Criticism happened to them, through a combination of luck, outrage, and moments in cities when building outstripped sense. There are strong parallels between the beginning of Huxtable's career as critic in the late 1950s and the building (and architecture) boom of the early twenty-first century. In both cases a certain amount of bedazzlement prevailed as glittering towers replaced brick-and-stucco neighborhoods. There were (and are) great pieces of architecture, but the speed of construction also fostered a culture of knock-offs—good ideas repeated in inhospitable places or with subpar materials.

Huxtable started her career as an assistant curator of architecture and design at the Museum of Modern Art (MoMA) in the 1940s. She received a Fulbright in 1950 to study modern architecture in Italy and subsequently wrote a book on architect and engineer Pier Luigi Nervi (*Pier Luigi Nervi*, published 1960). As one of few trained historians of the modern movement, she noticed gaps in the *New York Times*'s architecture coverage. Her sense of connoisseurship, distinguishing the best from the second-rate, served her from the very beginning of her career. In 1959 she wrote the *Times* editors a long letter in response to their positive review of a photography show on a modernist housing project in Caracas, Venezuela. Apparently, it looked great, but Huxtable had been there and had seen that the beautiful buildings did not work for their inhabitants. Her letter (printed in full) showed knowledge, passion, and a critical voice, and the paper hired her.

In 1963 Huxtable became the *New York Times*'s first architecture critic. She held that position, with variations in title, until 1982 and won a Pulitzer Prize in 1970. What is charming and replicable about her first ten years as reviewer is the immediacy of her experience of so many great works of modern architecture: the Whitney Museum, the CBS Building, the glass canyons of Park Avenue, the marble plazas of Lincoln Center. Reading her pieces (collected in the wonderfully and evocatively named *Kicked A Building Lately?* [1976] and *Will They Ever Finish Bruckner Boulevard?* [1970]), it is clear that her first loyalty is to the citizens of New York and that she thinks they deserve better.

Before she does anything else in "Sometimes We Do It Right," Huxtable describes what she sees. This may seem rather simplistic, but it is a step many critics skip today, since most reviews come with a photograph or slideshow. These writers want to leap over the visual to get to the big picture: the architect's genius, the international trend at work, the latent theory in the practice. Huxtable gives the reader explicit directions about where to stand and candidly states what she notices, offering immediate insight into reading a building or the city. First, you have to be there. Critiquing renderings is often a necessity, but you cannot gain insight into what works unless you have seen it, touched it, and experienced it in person. Here is the formal approach exemplified: she stands on the sidewalk and points you east.

> For a demonstration of New York at its physical best, go to Broadway between Cedar and Liberty Streets and face east. You will be standing in front of a new building at 140 Broadway....
>
> Look to your left (Liberty Street) and you will see the small turn-of-the-century French pastry in creamy, classically-detailed stone that houses the neighboring Chamber of Commerce. To your right (Cedar Street) is a stone-faced building of the first great skyscraper period (pre-World War I through the 1930's).
>
> Move on, toward the East River, following the travertine plaza that flows elegantly on either side of the slender new shaft, noting how well the block size of the marble under foot scales the space.

If you were to literally follow in her footsteps (as I hope you will), you would see just how much is not described in the text. The critic is an editor: to make a visual argument, you have to cut out much of what you see. You also have to comment on what you do see, as concisely as possible. Calling the Chamber of Commerce a "French pastry" is funny, conjuring up (for me) the idea of a croissant wedged between dour towers or artist Claes Oldenburg's 1965 *Proposed Colossal Monument for Park Avenue*, a Good Humor bar of sixty stories to replace the unloved Pan Am Building at the south end of the avenue. The Chamber of Commerce looks just as much like a crumpet today, with its fruity garlands and elaborate Ionic capitals, and still provides an excellent contrast in personality to both Marine Midland and the 1915 Equitable Building by Ernest R. Graham across Cedar Street.

Huxtable's allusion to the first skyscraper period is a historical reference that demonstrates her authority (she didn't see her first skyscraper yesterday) without interrupting the present-day flow. The "stone-faced" Equitable is a building distinguished less for its neoclassical wrapper than for its bulk: it fills its block from side to side and corner to corner. Its monstrous presence spurred the 1916 zoning resolution that sprinkled Manhattan's streets with tapered towers until it was revised in the 1960s to allow for slabs-with-plazas like Marine Midland. Equitable still looms larger than Marine Midland, despite being many floors shorter, because the open space around the later tower makes it seem slimmer—the rezoning was right.

The plaza at the south side of Marine Midland is edged with a planter and a series of benches, leading around the corner of Cedar Street to the lobby. From there, the plaza continues east toward the Chase Manhattan Bank Building, designed by Gordon Bunshaft for SOM seven years before he worked on Marine Midland. Your eye is led to and through the glass atrium that surrounds Chase's elevator core, as if you could see past it and on down Cedar Street. But your feet must stop. Nassau Street lies between 140 Broadway and Chase, and you can't move from one building's plaza to that of the next one without cutting between parked cars, crossing the street, going up some steps. A huge Chase logo looks like the end of the line.

> But the open space continues, even with this barrier [Nassau Street]. Closing it [Marine Midland's plaza] and facing Chase's gleaming 60-story tower across Liberty Street is the stony vastness of the 1924 Federal Reserve Building by York and Sawyer, its superscaled, cut limestone, Strozzi-type Florentine façade making a powerful play against Chase's bright aluminum and glass.

Huxtable stops here for a moment of sheer visual revelry. Her words are active, giving the architecture a sense of movement—*powerful play*, *gleaming*, *stony*— that allows a reader to feel what she feels for a moment. Most buildings do not move, but they have impact, and transmitting that impact verbally can fire the imaginations of people who might just have walked on by. These adjectives give a taste of the rhetorical explosion to come in the criticism of Muschamp. Huxtable has always been more reserved, but manages to give the buildings she describes personality through well-chosen descriptors. The Federal Reserve Building reads as stone wallpaper, so vast is its side, so crisply incised are its mortar joints. It is a model for

many of the postmodern office buildings built after Marine Midland, but its solidity
and strength are no longer achievable.

Huxtable then deploys another critic's trick, particularly useful for the
positive review, overstatement:

> This small segment of New York compares in effect and elegance with
> any celebrated Renaissance plaza or Baroque vista. The scale of the
> buildings, the use of open space, the views revealed or suggested, the
> contrasts of architectural style and material, of sculpted stone against
> satin-smooth metal and glass, the visible change and continuity of
> New York's remarkable skyscraper history, the brilliant accent of the
> poised Noguchi cube—color, size, style, mass, space, light, dark, solids,
> voids, highs and lows—all are just right.

It is hard to know if she really thinks this happenstance plaza beats those
in Rome and harder to believe many would agree with her. But her enthusiasm is
infectious and carries the reader to her larger point: cities are perpetually reinventing
themselves. We may prefer the uniformly ancient beauties of the Capitoline Hill,
but that is not a viable model for the contemporary city. Happenstance, accretion, a
change in neighbors can combine to create new beauty at any moment. The critic
would not be doing her job if she did not think today could be as good as the past.
And Huxtable, deeply involved in the preservation movement in New York City,
would not be doing her job if she did not recognize the qualities of older buildings
as well as the latest ones.

Her enthusiasm is as much for the historic as it is for Noguchi's then-
boldly-anarchic cube, which seems much larger in person than in photographs. That
cube is an interesting footnote. Today the corporate sculpture of the 1960s, much
of it by Noguchi, rarely warrants a second glance, so imitated has it been by lesser
sculptors, in lesser plazas. "Plop art" was the dismissive term coined by architect
James Wines in 1969 for large, geometric, and abstract sculptures in corporate
settings, suggesting that its commissioning and placement were too easy. It was as if
the corporate owners said to the people of New York, "Here you go, some Art." But

bad imitations should not lessen the impact of superior examples, and as Huxtable points out, the cube is just the right size, shape, and color, set just the right distance from the building.

One section of the review comes close to straight-up architecture criticism as we know it: the critic, the new building, an assessment:

> Not the least contribution is the new building, for which Gordon Bunshaft was partner-in-charge at S.O.M. One Forty Broadway is a "skin" building; the kind of flat, sheer, curtain wall that it has become chic to reject....
>
> It is New York's ultimate skin building. The wall is held unrelentingly flat; there are no tricks with projecting or extended mullions; thin or flush, they are used only to divide the window glass....The quiet assurance of this building makes even Chase look a little gaudy.

But this judgment of the curtain wall is only a fraction of what she has to say—she's rewritten her assignment on the fly, because the new building is the least of her concerns. In fact, Huxtable never says the building is good or bad but describes it in terms that make her appreciation clear. She gets inside the architecture by focusing almost exclusively on the curtain wall, as the curtain wall is what sets this box apart from its neighbors and the curtain wall is all that most members of the public will ever see of the building.

Ever since Bunshaft designed Lever House uptown on Park Avenue in 1952, New York's corporations had been involved in an endless game of curtain-wall one-upmanship. Thus, when Huxtable talks about flatness, she's describing the latest iteration in a search for new looks for the glass-and-steel tower. As Huxtable notes, by 1968 the public was growing as restless with this aesthetic as they were with plop art, but Marine Midland is a superior example of its type. The sense of collective urban ego present in the postwar building boom that produced so many skin buildings never happened in New York's last building boom, with the possible exception of the 2005 Hearst Tower by Foster + Partners. Huxtable sounds a prescient, doleful note in her conclusion: "What next? Probably destruction. One ill-conceived neighboring plaza will kill this carefully calculated channel of related space and buildings....It only takes one opening in the wrong place, one 'bonus' space placed according to current zoning (read 'business') practice to ruin it all."

"Sometimes We Do It Right" includes a number of features that I would urge readers of this book to use in their own writing. One, description: She sets the scene, and her theme, through opening paragraphs that bring the city vividly to mind. Two, history: She demonstrates that the skyscraper is not something new (via her neighborhood tour) and that Marine Midland is part of a lineage (via her discussion of curtain walls). These glancing references establish her expertise (she knows more about this topic than most) and also sidestep a common problem: a gee-whiz awe at the latest and greatest model in the line. Three, drama: Many people consider architecture boring. The first line of defense against this charge is making the connection for the reader between how architecture looks and how it makes one feel. It's not just a building but a speaking artifact. Finally, the Point: Huxtable has twelve hundred words with which to make her point. When you read her review, you feel at all times that she knows exactly where it is going. She has chosen the three areas she wants to highlight—the surroundings, the plaza, the building's skin— and she makes them with all deliberate speed. (If you have selected a theme and a mode of organization, and if you know what your critical approach is, having a point shouldn't be hard. Leave out more than you leave in.)

Huxtable's modest, carefully articulated rallying cry is left to the end: "Space is meaningless without scale, containment, boundaries and direction.... This is planning. It is the opposite of non-planning, or the normal patterns of New York development. See and savor it now, because it is carelessly disposed of." Her method is developmental, leading the reader to agreement rather than telling them what they will learn at the outset. Remember Huxtable's subtlety as you read the other examples in this book, and consider what they have in common: visual language, authority, argument. Huxtable is asking you to look at what is around the architecture as much as the building in question, calling your attention to what is really important to get right.

The more built environment people see and savor, the more they act like architecture critics, the better they will be able to recognize good planning and become advocates for it. What this book teaches is how to recognize, articulate, and argue for such continuing moments of beauty. The first step is following in the footsteps of the masters. The second is writing about the city you want to see.

House of Glass

LEWIS MUMFORD

New Yorker, AUGUST 8, 1952

PAGE 34

For a long time after Lever House opened its doors, throngs of people, waiting patiently in great queues in the lobby, demanded admission so insistently that the elevator system, designed to handle only Lever Brothers' office staff of twelve hundred employees and a normal complement of visitors, was severely overtaxed. People acted as if this was the eighth wonder of the world, this house of glass approached through an open forecourt that is paneled with glistening marble, punctuated by columns encased in stainless steel, and embellished by a vast bed of flowers and—last touch of elegance against the greenish-blue windows and the bluish-green spandrels of the glassy building that rises above it—a weeping-willow tree.

In many ways, this popular curiosity, which in a sense is also popular judgment, is justified. Lever House is a building of outstanding qualities, mechanical, aesthetic, human, and it breaks with traditional office buildings in two remarkable respects—it has been designed not for maximum rentability but for maximum efficiency in the dispatch of business, and it has used to the full all the means now available for making a building comfortable, gracious, and handsome. This whole structure is chastely free of advertisement; the minuscule glass cases showing life-size packages of Lever products in the glass-enclosed reception chamber on the ground floor would hardly be noticed in the lobby of a good hotel. But the building itself is a showcase and an advertisement; in its very avoidance of vulgar forms of publicity, it has become one of the most valuable pieces of advertising a big commercial

PAGE 35

enterprise could conceive. For years, businessmen vied with each other in the attempt to put up the tallest building in the city; thus the Metropolitan Life capped the Singer and the Empire State capped the Chrysler in the effort to make the sky the limit. In keeping with this now deplorably old-fashioned spirit, there have lately been rumors of a hundred-story skyscraper. Possibly Lever House has pointed the way for a new kind of competition—a competition to provide open spaces and a return to the human scale. At all events, it is definitely not an example of the "swaggering in specious dimensions" that [German historian and philosopher] Oswald Spengler called a sign of a decadent civilization.

PAGE 35

To understand what the architects of Lever House—Skidmore, Owings & Merrill, whose Gordon Bunshaft was chief designer—have achieved, one must go back to some of the buildings put up on midtown Madison Avenue in the early 'twenties. They are only twelve stories high, without setbacks, and they cover the entire site, providing not so much as an air shaft in the center. But though they have resulted in a heavier density of population than a wise zoning law would permit, they are immensely superior to the extravagant thirty- and forty-story buildings that followed them. So valuable have these older ones proved that one of them, 383 and 385 Madison Avenue, has now been completely renovated and given new elevators, an air-conditioning system, and numerous other embellishments at a cost as great as that of the building itself. Lever House returns to the more modest density achieved in this twelve-story structure. By not quite doubling that number of floors in the main part of their building, however, the architects of Lever House have been able to house those twelve hundred employees comfortably while providing an unusual amount of open space that is secure against encroachment. For the main structure, though it runs the cross-town length of the site and abuts the structure next door on the west, is set back a hundred feet from the south building line and forty from the north and has the generous width of Park Avenue to the east. The result of this self-discipline is that this shaft, or "slab," which is less than sixty feet wide, is open to the light on three sides, and few desks are more than twenty-five feet from the continuous windows. Even the least-favored worker on the premises may enjoy the psychological lift of raising her eyes to the clouds or the skyscape of not too near-at-hand adjoining buildings. I know no other private or public edifice in the city that provides space of such quality for every worker.

The layout of this building is itself transparent. The tall, narrow, oblong slab, which houses the firm's offices, is set off-center on a roughly square pedestal, only two stories high, that covers the whole plot, the western block front along Park Avenue between Fifty-third and Fifty-fourth. This irregularly shaped site runs a hundred and fifty-five feet west on Fifty-third and a hundred and ninety feet west on Fifty-fourth. The pedestal is a hollow one, for there is a court open to the sky in the middle of it, just to the south of the slab. To the north of the court, on the ground floor, is the glass-walled main lobby, and to the west of the court are an auditorium and a kitchen laboratory. The court, and the lobby, can be reached from almost any direction, for the ground floor is completely open on three sides—north, south, and east—to the streets; there is no vestige of wall, or even of shop-front window, to shut out the passer-by. The second floor contains, among other things, an employees' lounge, handsomely done in dark green and mustard yellow, and a spacious room that houses the stenographers' pool. The third story, the beginning of the slab, contains a kitchen and cafeteria, which can feed all hands in two and a half hours; this dining room, with its reddish-brown drapes and modern furniture, is able to hold its own in elegance with any restaurant on Park Avenue, and it has something that no restaurant in the city has offered since the old beer gardens disappeared—a thickly planted open-air roof garden that flanks it (and, of course, the slab) on both north and south. If it weren't for its almost hepatic sound, the word "Leverish" might well take the place of "ritzy" as a synonym for the last word in luxury. This floor of the slab is indented a whole bay along the Park Avenue side, so the rest of the slab seems to hover over the base of the structure. The indentation permits the bed of plants that borders the roof garden to be carried without interruption along this entire frontage of the building. Unfortunately, the bay is not deep enough to permit people as well as plants to make this journey from south to north. Thus no one can take a full turn on the roof-garden deck, and the architects' sacrifice of free promenade space to the unbroken bed of greenery must be set down as a

PAGE 36

piece of empty formalism—all the worse aesthetically because the movement of people across the front of the building would have given an extra touch of life to a somewhat glacial, if not oversimplified, composition. This seems to me a blemish, but it is not beyond remedy.

The office building proper ends with the executives' offices, on the twenty-first floor. Above them are three floors, outwardly punctuated by the horizontal louvers of the air intakes, behind which are the elevator machinery and a cooling tank. All this is surrounded by a shell strong enough to support the elaborate machine that moves around the perimeter of the roof to raise and lower the window cleaners' platform. This piece of apparatus was necessitated by the fact that the entire slab, windows and spandrels alike, is— except, as has already been pointed out, on the west side—sheathed in glass, and the windows are all sealed. The windows are four and a half feet wide, and even the smallest private office has two of them. For a company whose main products are soap and detergents, that little handicap of the sealed windows is a heaven-sent opportunity, for what could better dramatize its business than a squad of cleaners operating in their chariot, like the deus ex machina of Greek tragedy, and capturing the eye of the passer-by as they perform their daily duties? This perfect bit of symbolism alone almost justifies the all-glass facade.

PAGE 37

The slab is the traditional steel-framed skyscraper, with one or two special features. The outer columns are set back a little from the outer walls, so the windows are a continuous glassy envelope, and the mechanical core of the building—the passenger elevators, the conveyor that delivers outgoing mail to the postal department and incoming mail to the proper floors, the coat racks for the office force, the fire stairs—is concentrated in the west end of the slab. If necessary, therefore, a wing could be built south from this end, parallel to Park Avenue, without taking away any daylight from the existing working quarters. The only opaque feature in this house of glass is that demanded by prudence and the fire ordinances of New York—the fire stairs, which are enclosed in a shaft of light-gray brick at the west side of the site and connected with the slab by open passages at each floor level. At the base of the fire tower is the entrance to the fifty-five-car underground garage for the staff.

Aesthetically, the exterior of this building has a sober elegance; the stainless-steel window frames and spandrel frames are repeated without variation over the whole facade. The darker bands of the spandrels give horizontal emphasis, while the gleam of the vertical metal framing, sometimes reinforced by the columns behind, provides a delicate counterpoise. The effect is of alternating bands of dark-green and light-green glass, and, as is true of all glass buildings, this surface looks far darker than it would if an opaque covering, such as white brick, had been used. Paradoxically, a whole city of such buildings, so open to light, would be somber, since a transparent glass wall is mostly light-absorbing, not light-reflecting. When the framing of Lever House was put up, it was protected by a coating of brilliant chrome-yellow paint, and though the cost of maintaining this brilliance might have been prohibitive, that chrome yellow, playing against the green, would have given the building a gaiety it lacks. Standing by itself, reflecting the nearby buildings in its mirror surface, Lever House presents a startling contrast to the old-fashioned buildings of Park Avenue. But if its planning innovations prove sound, it may become just one unit in a repeating pattern of buildings and open spaces.

PAGE 35

The uniformity and the severity of the exterior glass-and-metal envelope do not characterize the interior of the building, for in its decoration this severity has been richly humanized. This decor was designed and executed by Raymond Loewy Associates. Just as a sensible farmer designs his cow stalls around his cow, the fundamental unit around which Lever House's hundred and thirty thousand square feet of floor space was designed was the desk. The desks in the working quarters are of adjustable height and have rounded corners, to reduce the number of nylon snags. To offset the bluish light from the exterior, a grayish beige was chosen as the basic color for desks and floors. (Even the elevator boys are dressed in dark beige.) But against that background a great variety of colors has been introduced. Each floor has its own color scheme, from brisk yellows and delicate blues to a combination—on the floor devoted to the firm's cosmetics—of boudoir pink and eyeshadow lavender. I don't know any other building in the city in which so much color has been used with such skill and charm over such a large area. Both our school architects and our equally timid hospital architects have something to learn from this.

PAGE 37

There is only one dismal flaw in the excellence of the interior decoration; this occurs on the topmost floor, sacred to the chief executives. Here nothing has been spared to achieve an air of expensiveness, and as a result nothing more stuffy and depressing could be imagined. Instead of the clean, shapely clocks that tell the time on the lower floors, there is a fussy, ornamented clock, set in a frame of golden rays; instead of bright-colored hangings and coverings, a drab plushiness, doubtless intended to symbolize solidity, power, and wealth, has the effect of expressing timidity and the spirit of retreat—in contrast to the forthright confidence and gaiety of the rest of the building. Why this descent from the era of stainless steel and glass to the nether regions of the Brown Decades? Is this a last desperate gesture toward the good old days, when income and corporation taxes and unemployment insurance and welfare plans did not exist? The clean logic of the whole building is denied by this executives' floor. The way to symbolize leadership and responsibility is not to give executives a duller kind of decoration than their subordinates but to give them precisely the same kind, if on a more generous scale of space.

PAGE 37

Because Lever House has many points in common with the United Nations Secretariat, it is inevitable that the buildings should be compared. On almost every point, it seems to me, Lever House is superior. To begin with, it is correctly oriented, with its wide facades facing north and south, and though this means that no direct sunlight ever enters the northern windows, it also means that there is no need to cut light and view on that side by drawing Venetian blinds. Since there are three air-conditioning systems—for the north side, the south side, and the middle—in the winter, warm air can be introduced on the cool side of the building while cooler air is circulated on the sunny side. The United Nations cafeteria for employees is good, but the one in Lever House ranks with the quarters provided not for the U.N. staff but for the executives and delegates. And there is no open space around the Secretariat that compares in charm and comfort with Lever House's courtyard and roof garden, enclosed as these are on two sides.

Few of the features that make Lever House superior are the result of its having a more generous budget to draw on. Though they are superficially similar, one may say of these buildings that the United Nations is the last of the old-fashioned skyscrapers, in which importance was symbolized by height, while Lever House is the first of the new office buildings, in which the human needs and purposes modify cold calculations of profit and nullify any urge to tower above rival buildings. In Lever House, quality of space takes precedence over mere quantity.

The building that Lever House really invites comparison with is quite a different structure, though equally bold and even more striking architecturally in its own day—Frank Lloyd Wright's now demolished Larkin Building, in Buffalo, the paragon of office buildings at the time, though set in the midst of an industrial slum it never succeeded in dominating or even modifying. It, too, was a by-product of the soap industry. In that building, as in this one, every possible innovation was made—new desks, new chairs, new office equipment of every kind, all of it specially designed. The Larkin Building was a shallow structure, built about a great skylighted interior court, with natural light coming down through the roof. Wright's creation was a masterpiece of beautiful masonry—more monumental, in fact, than most public buildings, whether churches or city halls, that have sought to be. Lever House lacks the massive sculptural qualities of Wright's inspired masonry; it is, rather, in its proud transparency, "a construction in space." It says all that can be said, delicately, accurately, elegantly, with surfaces of glass, with ribs of steel, with an occasional contrast in slabs of marble or in beds of growing plants, but its special virtues are most visible not in the envelope but in the interior that this envelope brings into existence, in which light and space and color constitute both form and decoration. In terms of what it set out to do, this building— excluding the deplorable executives' floor and the wall encrusted with golden mosaic that faces one in approaching the elevators on the ground floor—is an impeccable achievement. Lever Brothers and Skidmore, Owings & Merrill, and above all Gordon Bunshaft, are entitled to a civic vote of thanks for taking this important step toward sane planning and building. Lever House is not, of course, the first all-glass building; the famous Crystal Palace, and the more recent Daily Express Building, on Fleet Street, in London, antedate it. But it is the first office building in which modern materials, modern construction, modern functions have been combined with a modern plan. In a sense, it picks up the thread where the architects of the Monadnock Building in Chicago, the last of the ail-masonry skyscrapers, dropped it two generations ago.

On the surface, this seems about the best that current architecture can provide when limitations of cost do not, in any substantial way, enter into the picture. It will be a little while before one can make a final appraisal of this building; that will depend partly upon how comfortable the quarters have been in the summer and how expensive it has been to keep them comfortable, likewise on how satisfactory this building will be in very cold weather. It is a show place and an advertisement, and costs that can here be written off to publicity might prove too high for more workaday business quarters. Though the uniform facade of Lever House is aesthetically consistent, a different system of fenestration on the south side, with or without sun screens, might not merely produce better summer temperatures within but might also reduce the need for shutting off the view with Venetian blinds, a necessity that makes nonsense of the windows. It may be, too, that a more flexible system of ventilation, which depended more frequently on untreated air and would use air-conditioning only to counteract extreme temperatures, would prove more satisfactory as well as cheaper. And in that event Lever House's closed-in glass face, along with its amusing window-cleaning apparatus, could be discarded in newer designs. Surely no building so open to the direct rays of the sun—particularly the valuable ultraviolet rays of morning—should nullify that advantage by "windows" that do not let these rays in. But Lever House, by reason of the internal consistency in its design, is at the very least a highly useful experiment. Fragile, exquisite, undaunted by the threat of being melted into a puddle by an atomic bomb, this building is a laughing refutation of "imperialist warmongering," and so it becomes an implicit symbol of hope for a peaceful world. In the kind of quarters it provides for its staff, Lever House even anticipates the "Century of the Common Man." I don't know whether that is what the corporation had in mind when it built this structure, but that, it seems to me, is what Lever House itself says.

PAGE 38

CHAPTER 1

SKYSCRAPERS AS SUPERLATIVES

"Something new under the sun." That's what Louis Sullivan called the tall office building in 1896. He recognized the type as the major project for architects of the twentieth century, one which evolved as steel frames replaced masonry structure and elevators upended traditional ideas of spatial hierarchy. By the turn of the century, the penthouse, rather than the piano nobile, had become the most desirable real estate. In many of the earliest examples (architect-engineer William LeBaron Jenney is usually credited with the first skyscraper, the Home Insurance Building of 1885 in Chicago), the outline of the first floor was simply multiplied upward as high as steel and the Otis elevator, patented in 1854, could go. Skyscrapers—recognized as the first native American architectural type—soon proliferated in other downtowns across the United States, sprung from the "social conditions" of urban density, business growth, and new technology. Buildings of common purpose and features appeared in Chicago, New York, Buffalo, St. Louis—less products of artistry than of industry.

From the beginning the skyscraper was defined by superlatives. As business propositions each building had to sell itself to prospective tenants in the language of advertising: the type was new, but each speculative tower was the newest, the tallest, the largest. As the number of skyscrapers increased, the means of distinguishing one from the next also needed to grow in an arms race to garner publicity and appeal to the best tenants. By the turn of the century, and the publication of Louis Sullivan's essay "The Tall Office Building Artistically Considered" (1896), that arms race needed to add "most beautiful" to the arsenal. Sullivan saw that square footage was no longer enough and cities were suffering from blocks put up merely to achieve real-estate goals. He was one of the first to identify what could make one skyscraper aesthetically superior to the next and in doing so created a basic checklist for any criticism (beyond price) of the type. Mumford's "House of Glass" did the same for the first important innovation for American skyscrapers since 1896: the curtain wall, which swept aside historical ornament and traditional layout with glass and open-plan offices, respectively.

Today the competition of superlatives continues. The primary focus of this chapter is "House of Glass," longtime *New Yorker* architecture critic Lewis Mumford's 1952 review of Lever House, the first all-glass skyscraper built in New York City after World War II. But the larger lesson is the continuity in criticism, from 1896 to the present day, of the search for something new in architecture via the skyscraper. Sullivan anatomized the parts of the tall office building, showing us the structure beneath the stone or glass or metal skins. Mumford shows us how Lever House rewrites those rules, setting a different sort of standard than the race for the sky epitomized by the Chrysler and Empire State buildings. Sullivan's ideal skyscrapers are freestanding sculptures, while Mumford's have to work on specific sites, offer public open spaces and daylit offices, and be symbols of American optimism. So powerful was Lever's example that when, in 2006, the Hearst Tower by Foster + Partners opened on Eighth Avenue in New York City, Paul Goldberger harked back to a descendent of Lever House to amplify his praise in "Triangulation" (*New Yorker*, December 19, 2005). Hearst also offered an open base, a brand-new transparent facade, and a new beginning after a wounding event (the destruction of the World Trade Center on September 11, 2001). But it also added the latest –est: greenest.

Superlatives are the *theme* of this chapter—tallest, friendliest, greenest—illustrating the importance of choosing a stance as well as a subject. In analyzing Mumford's review, I discuss his *organization* and the path of the sidewalk critic. Finally, in the contrast between the prose of Sullivan, Mumford, and Goldberger—the words they use, the emphasis they give to the architect and to other buildings—there is a clear differentiation in *approach* to the whole matter of architectural criticism.

Among the first to write about the cultural meaning of the skyscraper was Sullivan, in his justly famous "The Tall Office Building Artistically Considered." Sullivan wrote from the perspective of a designer, having completed two short, almost-cubic buildings, in Buffalo and St. Louis, that then qualified as skyscrapers: "Problem: How shall we impart to this sterile pile, this crude, harsh, brutal agglomeration, this stark, staring exclamation of eternal strife, the graciousness of those higher forms of sensibility and culture that rest on the lower and fiercer passions?"

His question has still not been entirely answered. Since Sullivan the advances of technology and commerce have pushed the inventiveness of architects onward and upward, with the balance between crudity and sensibility always changing. Races to the top occurred in 1931, when the brutal Empire State Building topped the elegant Chrysler Building; in 1974 when the agglomerative Sears Tower topped the stark World Trade Center; and, the timeline speeding up, the Petronas Towers in 1998 in Kuala Lumpur, Taipei 101 in 2004, the Shanghai World Financial Center in 2008, and the Burj Khalifa in 2010 in Dubai. Even as Sullivan defined the tall office building by its height, he sought means to make it speak visually of its function and to create a replicable, recognizable framework for its form. What's particularly interesting about this essay is Sullivan's struggle to find a language for the skyscraper both as a critic and as an architect.

Sullivan was motivated by the belief that architects follow rather than lead. The process of building towers was driven, then as it is now, by speculators (developers), engineers, and builders—the architect asked to dress a box created by others. Sullivan wanted architects to take control of the process, creating integrated works of art rather than applying a wallpaper of outdated architectural styles.

Previous types, like churches, courthouses, schools, and palaces, had developed distinct architectural language over centuries. In a new town, the building with a bell tower was always a church; the building with columns, the town hall (or the post office). It was a grammar with which most were familiar.

Skyscrapers threw that grammar into confusion. Were the new buildings "cathedrals of commerce" that should be clad in Gothic ornament? If they included banks, should they take on the prominent colonnades? Or were they more like industrial plants, space enclosed cheaply and with minimal decoration? What was (and is) the essence of the skyscraper as a type? The answer to Sullivan was immediately obvious: "It is lofty. This loftiness is to the artist-nature its thrilling aspect. It is the very open organ-tone in its appeal. It must be in turn the dominant chord in the expression of it, the true excitant of his imagination. It must be tall, every inch of it tall."

Sullivan could have stopped right there. This idea of tallness was, in 1896, something new. The first skyscrapers were not tall, in reality or in concept. Jenney's Home Insurance Building, for example, is divided horizontally into a grid of one- to three-story sections, each one resembling a small, solid, and vaguely classical office building of old. This was precisely, in Sullivan's view, what a tall office building should not look like, as they were not meant to be a display of all previous architectural knowledge: "A sixteen story building must not consist of sixteen separate, distinct and unrelated buildings piled one upon the other until the top of the pile is reached." Sullivan's own earlier designs, the Wainwright Building (1891) in St. Louis and the Guaranty Building (1895) in Buffalo, verge on tallness. The body of the Guaranty Building, above the first two commercial floors, is striated with vertical terra-cotta mullions set in front of the horizontal spandrels below the windows. These strips emphasize the height of the building and end in a series of graceful arches just below the building's heavy cap. To the contemporary eye, this cap robs the building of upward momentum.

Looking at skyscraper examples of the previous thirty years, Sullivan examines them for signs of a common language. He finds that every building has a basement, unseen and below ground, containing boilers, the steam plant, and other building systems. Above that, a first floor with an entrance for all tenants, made attractive with a large opening and public access to stores and banks. Above that "an indefinite number of offices piled tier upon tier, one tier just like another tier, one office just like all the other offices." Sullivan's revelation of the replicability of the office floors—that they did not need to be distinguished one from another—is one of the most modern insights in his essay. The idea of the sameness of the program of most floors of office buildings, expressed in his design for Guaranty, was interpreted over and over during the twentieth century—from the sheer glass walls of Mies van der Rohe's slabs to the saw-toothed diagrid of Hearst Tower. Atop these innumerable floors of office cells was the attic, a space occupied with the mechanics of heating, cooling, and lighting. Because the attic is visible, however, Sullivan gave it symbolic weight, broadness, prominence in order to say "that the series of office tiers has come definitely to an end." He adds that from these programmatic divisions "results, naturally, spontaneously, unwittingly, a three-part division, not from any theory, symbol, or fancied logic."

Earlier in the essay, Sullivan pointed out a number of theories others had applied to the skyscraper: it should be treated as a column, divided into base, shaft, and capital; it should be treated as a logical statement, with beginning, middle, and end; it should be treated as a mystical symbol that always come in threes (for example, morning, noon, night). That trees, the basis for any organic design, are divided into roots, trunk, and limbs. (In 1931, Sullivan's protégé Frank Lloyd Wright would design a skyscraper based structurally on a tree, with a long taproot, a pinwheeling shaft of identical apartments, and flaring top foliage.) But to Sullivan these philosophical explanations are unnecessary: "All things in nature have a shape, that is to say, a form, an outward semblance, that tells them what they are, that distinguishes them from ourselves and from each other. Unfailing in nature these shapes express the inner life, the native quality of animal, tree, bird, fish, that they present to us; they are so characteristic, so recognizable, that we say, simply, it is 'natural' it should be so." For Sullivan the same is true of the building and his utilitarian diagram is enough of an underpinning for art. He writes, in words that would be echoed by modern architects in the century to come: "Form ever follows function." Sullivan provided the basic template by which all subsequent skyscrapers would need to be evaluated. When you critique a skyscraper today, you could do much worse than to ask Sullivan's questions: Is it tall? Does it differentiate its functions visually? Does it have an inner life, a personality, character? The answers to these questions help to zero in on a theme, what's special to know and discuss about your particular skyscraper.

While Sullivan sits at his drafting board, Mumford stands across the street from the building. He has no tools beyond his eyes, no access beyond that of the interested citizen. What is important to Mumford is what is important to his readers: What does it look like? How does it introduce itself? What does it mean? Sullivan's essay on the skyscraper sets up a checklist for the architect; Mumford puts that checklist into practice. His review discusses the building from lobby to top, its presence on the skyline and its presence on the street, but he adds the element of physical experience. The skyscraper for Mumford is not a piece of sculpture but part of the urban organism, changing pedestrian patterns, changing the weather on a given street, changing the way a city sees itself.

Mumford's approach was self-invented, just as his education in architecture was self-determined. Mumford went to Stuyvesant High School in Manhattan, then started at City College in philosophy. During the 1910s he spent time on the streets of New York, drawing and noting the change in the city during its first skyscraper boom. He was asked to take over the Sky Line column in the *New Yorker* in 1931 after writing an essay for the *New Republic* in which he called Rockefeller Center, just completed, "the sorriest failure of imagination and intelligence in modern American architecture." (One of the pleasures of reading historical architecture critiques is finding that universally beloved buildings weren't so popular the first time around.) Mumford always thought of himself as a social critic and philosopher. Architecture was part of that research, but Mumford perceived it as a limited field. In "House of Glass," however, the philosopher and the man on the street came together. The review is about much more than a skyscraper, and he approaches the building not from above but from the ground, and not as an expert but as part of the excited crowd: "People acted as if this was the eighth wonder of the world."

Lever House is a slim, 24-story slab, 306 feet high, whose shaft—shifted to the north side of the block—begins at the second floor. It was designed by Gordon

Bunshaft of Skidmore, Owings & Merrill (SOM), the firm that would become synonymous with tall office buildings that came after Lever House. The second floor is the only one to fill the block from sidewalk to sidewalk, and consists of a pizza box–like form, with a hole cut out of the center. Poking out over the top of the box are hedges that border the employees' garden adjacent to the cafeteria. The whole building is covered in a skin of green-tinted glass, clear at window height, opaque below it, and shiny stainless-steel mullions divide the panes. The ground level is open, except for the transparent glass–enclosed lobby directly under the tower.

In a 1957 article titled "The Park Avenue School of Architecture," Ada Louise Huxtable named Lever House the original of this school of building: "Lever Brothers' trend-setting green glass tower…established the vogue for glass walled buildings and was soon flanked by imitations." The revolution Lever offered was threefold: it brought European modernism to New York; it created a new, public-spirited office type; and it transformed an outmoded street into a cohesive urban experience. Mumford predicted this transformative aspect right away: "If its planning innovations prove sound, it may become just one unit in a repeating pattern of buildings and open spaces."

The space notched out of the skyscrapers built on Park and Sixth avenues makes it possible for a pedestrian to get out of the flow and actually look at the buildings. The curtain walls became the part of the building that expressed its message. The open court, the weeping willow in a planter box, the fishbowl lobby suggest to Mumford the beginning of "a new competition to provide open spaces and a return to the human scale." The word *competition* is key to Mumford's critique: Lever House changed the rules of the skyscraper game. "For years, businessmen vied with each other in the attempt to put up the tallest building in the city," he writes, and loftiness was all. That competition was really a form of advertising: being the tallest provoking the repetition of the company name, provoking free publicity at the opening. In Lever's case, such decadent and antiurban showmanship was unnecessary. It didn't need to be the tallest, because it was the best: "The building itself is a showcase and an advertisement; in its very avoidance of vulgar forms of publicity, it has become one of the most valuable pieces of advertising a big commercial enterprise could conceive."

Mumford does a lot in the space of two paragraphs. The opening welcomes the reader as part of the crowd and positions him or her next to Mumford on the crowded sidewalk. This begins his organizational strategy, to walk the reader through the building, step by step, describing as he goes. The second paragraph speaks to his big-picture theme, Lever House as a new form of skyscraper, perfect for that moment. He is examining this building but also all previous buildings of this type. Lever both acknowledges and dispenses with the tripartite division. It replaces the grand entrance and public shops with a modest revolving door. In the lobby the functions are reduced to the essential: door, desk, elevator. Above that open plaza, the change in function to the second-floor cafeteria is expressed in the shape of the broad box. Above that, the office cells repeat in the simplest possible form: the rectangle. On top, there is no crown. Lever House was not going to enter that competition. Its innovation, its —est, was in the curtain wall: its transparency and simplicity was its billboard, its advertisement.

Mumford's reviews were never accompanied by photographs, so he had to provide the entire architectural experience with words. This is a worthwhile exercise even today, as photography is not an unmediated experience—it can exalt and distort three-dimensional space—and you never know where a piece of writing will end up. To allow the reader to "see" the building your way is one of the strengths of a written critique. Photographs offer the vision of the photographer and/or the editor who makes the selection. Words are the critic's own. By calling attention, as Huxtable does, to the historical architecture around the Marine Midland Building or by stressing, as Mumford does, the accessibility of the court, the critic can emphasize what he or she thinks are the most important elements. "The court, and the lobby, can be reached from almost any direction, for the ground floor is completely open on three sides—north, south, and east—to the streets; there is no vestige of wall, or even of shop-front window, to shut out the passer-by."

Mumford has already called the building "this house of glass" and the layout "transparent." This description of the way one enters the building is factual but also emphasizes these qualities. The building is open, which is important in ways he discusses later on, but it is also literally commercial-free. Unlike other companies that built bigger than their needs—and rented out floors to other enterprises or filled their lobbies with shops—Lever has decided to leave itself alone. The then-startling starkness of the all-glass facade was not compromised by advertising, and neither was its first floor. Mumford notes with regret that none of the windows are operable (as the rise of the skyscraper paralleled the invention of the elevator, so the rise of the all-glass skyscraper paralleled the invention of air-conditioning) and remarks on some drama resulting from the exterior's "uniformity and severity": the deus ex machina of the window-washing gondola, cleaning the glass with fine Lever Brothers products.

Inside Lever House, Mumford's standards change. He continues the walking tour but considers the inside as a place to work rather than a public and symbolic statement. His focus shrinks in scale from the curtain wall to the desk. Again, his narrative organization controls what the reader "sees" of Lever House's 130,000 square feet designed around the desk.

Mumford's one harsh critique is of the executive floors, where the modernity of the exterior and of the employee floors has been abandoned, "and as a result nothing more stuffy and depressing could be imagined." Executives continued to wall themselves up with wood paneling while their employees got linoleum, glass partitions, plastics. They had the will to restructure their companies, rebuild their headquarters, but quailed at the idea that they might have to remake themselves. The paragraph about the topmost floor gives Mumford a chance to try some dry humor and acts as a tonic for the overwhelmingly positive tone of the review.

Unrelenting praise can be dull and hard to believe without the many specifics details and comparisons Mumford includes. Words like *beautiful* and *elegant* don't register without an explanation of why this curtain wall is more elegant than that one, this stone pavement more beautiful because of its texture, or pattern, or something else. Writers need to include some pepper along with the sugar of praise. Mentioning what he does not like assures the reader that Mumford has not been lulled into a false sense of comfort. His eye is still sharp, even when it likes what it sees.

In the final paragraphs of "House of Glass" Mumford returns to the historical precedents he raised in the first. Mumford mourns the lack of monumentality in Lever House, too light to be compared to a cathedral, but sees that transparency is the future of architecture. Transparency serves as an up-to-date version of the symbolism that encrusted the old-school skyscraper, from the 1913 Woolworth Building's ecclesiastical Gothic terra cotta to the 1930 Chrysler Building's silvery hood-ornament gargoyles. Here Mumford veers into the mode of cultural historian, seeking the larger truth embedded in Lever House's popularity. At the beginning of the review, he suggested its modesty might start a new humanist trend. By the end he sees it as nothing less than a rebuke of Cold War attitudes. The United Nations Secretariat, completed two years before, should have been a symbol of democracy at work but failed in its emblematic task. Mumford, having thoroughly enumerated the building's virtues as advertisement and as workplace, can now turn his mind to its meaning.

After Lever, the deluge. Lever got an even more elegant neighbor, Mies van der Rohe's Seagram Building (1958), catty-corner across the street. The postwar boom required so much building and that building up seemed to be so entirely in glass, that by the late 1960s the style had been exhausted. Modernists began to investigate concrete and stone; postmodernism returned the skyscraper to the pastiche of historic architectural language Sullivan had mocked. Skyscrapers continued to be built, but until the fall of the World Trade Center on September 11, 2001, they had become urban wallpaper. Mumford's utopian words came to seem sadly prescient, and again the tall office building became freighted with meaning.

The building that stepped into this history—and proved to be a worthy vehicle for formal, historical, and symbolic writing—is Foster + Partners' Hearst Tower. Almost all the building's reviews reached for comparisons to the storied modernist past begun by Lever House (now rebranded as the *Mad Men* era), typically through to its last embodiments, the 1967 Ford Foundation by Kevin Roche John Dinkeloo & Associates and the Marine Midland Building, in order to put Hearst into context. The goals for the building, if not its muscular aesthetic, seemed in alignment: new technologies, an advanced curtain wall, a symbol of defiance in the face of terror. Like Lever, it was a showcase and an advertisement, this time for sustainable architecture and the design bona fides of its owner, the Hearst Corporation, a magazine and newspaper publisher. It was a building that meant more than a building. Like Lever House, it plays with Sullivan's organic tripartite division and is without the skyscraper's traditional crown.

Goldberger's approach to reviewing the skyscraper, and to architecture review in general, couldn't be more opposed to that of Mumford. Goldberger typically starts with the man, not the building, and turns the structure in question into an exemplar of the work of the architect. (Huxtable, Sullivan, and Mumford barely mention the architects, so focused are they on the form of the artifact.) The urban and pedestrian experience are secondary—there may not even be space in the review for a walk-through—as Goldberger is more interested in identifying the players on the international architectural stage. Goldberger's review of the Hearst Tower, "Triangulation," succinctly demonstrates his method, beginning with the architect himself:

> Norman Foster is the Mozart of modernism. He is nimble and prolific, and his buildings are marked by lightness and grace. He works very hard, but his designs don't show the effort. He brings an air of unnerving aplomb to everything he creates—from skyscrapers to airports, research laboratories to art galleries, chairs to doorknobs. His ability to produce surprising work that doesn't feel labored must drive his competitors crazy.

This opening sets a mood and a tone—happy, efficient, designed for big business—that applies equally well to Foster as it does to Hearst. After this breezy introduction, Goldberger follows with a capsule history of Foster's career, stressing the skyscrapers that, at the time he was writing, bookended Foster's career. That out of the way, he turns to the building at hand. His description of Foster's solution to the tricky problem of building on top of Joseph Urban's 1920s Hearst headquarters ("six stories of megalomaniacal pomp") is filled with action words, harking back to the *nimble, grace,* and *aplomb* in the opening paragraph. The key visual is "a shiny missile shooting out of Urban's launching pad," an image simultaneously vigorous and vulgar, evocative and bizarre. Do we want our skyscrapers to be weapons of mass destruction? Goldberger goes on to describe Foster's design process as a similar mix of violence and inspiration: "Foster started with a box, then sliced off the corners and ran triangles up and down the sides, pulling them in and out—a gargantuan exercise in nip and tuck."

What is clear is that the shaft of the building, those identical offices, are the design's singular statement. As at Lever House, its offspring, the once-plain center of the tripartite composition, now bears the weight of symbolism and superlatives. But is Goldberger really *describing* here? Without the photo, could you visualize the Hearst building? He sketches the process of design in cinematic (rather than realistic) terms and anthropomorphizes the building. But he doesn't really tell you what, how, where with Mumford's slow pace.

The original Urban building was meant as the base—grand entrance, shops, street identity—for a shaft and crown to be completed later. The plan to build up was halted by the Great Depression, and in the seventy years that followed, Hearst simply grew the company in rented, noncontiguous spaces. Urban's early career had been in stage design, and his building looks as if he had tried to invent a classical order for a fictional king out of whole cloth (which makes sense, given that his client was William Randolph Hearst, who had a kingly castle at San Simeon in California). For the historicist architect there would be no way to "match" the original. The crusading modern architect would have insisted it be torn down. The safe option would have been an undistinguished tower in a similar beige stone. But contemporary theories of preservation, which seek to emphasize the difference between old buildings and new ones, suggest Foster's solution: a new building, every inch of it new, which preserves the DNA of the old without any form of imitation. As Goldberger writes,

> Joseph Urban's goal in the original Hearst Building was to create a respectable form of flamboyance, and Foster has figured out how to do the same thing with his tower, in unquestionably modern terms, and without compromising his commitment to structural innovation. Foster is at his best when solving puzzles like this one; unlike most elite architects, he isn't obsessed with creating his own pure forms.

Goldberger puts Foster's own structural flamboyance in historical context: Foster is not the only one with the idea of external, diamond-pattern structure, and Goldberger theorizes that he has "matched" Urban in spirit. Then Goldberger writes, "Indeed, the Hearst tower is the most beautiful skyscraper to go up in New York since 1967, when SOM completed the stunningly serene 140 Broadway, in Lower Manhattan." This big comparison (most beautiful in almost forty years!) is accompanied by another when, in the last column of the review, Goldberger finally takes us inside. Up until now, he has told us a lot about Foster, some about the site history and design idea, and described in emotional terms the look of the tower. User experience is secondary, despite the fact that Goldberger has further history-minded praise for what Foster has done with the interior: "What comes next is an explosive surprise such as has not been seen in the city since Frank Lloyd Wright led people through a low, tight lobby into the rotunda of the Guggenheim. The escalators deposit you in a vast atrium that contains the upper floors of the old Urban building, which Foster has carved out and roofed over with glass."

More action words, more illustrious forbearers. Goldberger is selling us Foster as the contemporary king of the tower—the details don't matter much. Sullivan tried to demystify the design process of the skyscraper, but Goldberger reapplies the fairy dust.

Along with his cursory look at the building's interior and exterior, Goldberger also glosses over the Hearst Tower's other superlative: greenest. Hearst was eventually LEED Gold-certified. By the end of the 2000s, this level of sustainability was necessary for any large office complex, and rivals like the Bank of America Tower at One Bryant Park (2009) by Cook + Fox aimed for Platinum certification. In 2006 Hearst was the first in the former category and received a lot of media attention for the way green design and great design had been woven together. Foster's diagrid uses 20 percent less steel than a comparable orthogonal design, and 90 percent of the steel in the building is recycled material, including waste from the interior demolition of the Urban building. Today the occupied building is attempting to produce zero waste. The waterfall sculpture in the lobby—the secure equivalent of Lever's open plaza—is fed by rainwater and humidifies that vast space.

Goldberger's review shows that Hearst is a worthy successor to Lever in the design department but fails to address the ways in which Foster and his clients have also taken up its ideological slant, standing up to terror and acting as an instruction manual for enlightened corporatism. The loss of public plaza is a function of that terror environment. Perhaps the elimination of open space is made up for by the building's conservation. Hearst too requires specially designed window-washing gondolas, but their promotional potential is limited by the fact that Hearst does not make soap. Hearst's product is publicity, and given the continuing level of interest in the building and its critical reputation above those of rival media companies like Condé Nast and the New York Times (who also built green office towers in Manhattan in the 2000s), it too succeeds as an advertisement without words.

The skyscraper's identity has always been wrapped up with symbolism. It is the building type with the most obvious literary qualities and the possibility for use of the most experimental language. Remember how Sullivan searched simultaneously for a written and a built language for the tall building? When we think of architects and buildings, it is often of skyscrapers we first think.

This chapter presented three exemplary approaches to the skyscraper: as design problem, as symbol, and as personification. Each of the reviews discussed literally approaches the building from a different angle: Sullivan from within, Mumford from without, Goldberger from biography. But each critic makes his theme clear from the outset and pursues it to the end, organizing his critique as an argument, asking and answering questions introduced in the first paragraphs. Sullivan's analytical approach may take him from the building's utilities to the ideal classical column, but the idea of the tall building, the expression of loftiness, is present from start to finish. Mumford makes it clear that he is evaluating Lever House for two publics, its client (and the client's employees) and the general public, and methodically pursues its excellence from the sidewalk to the executive suite, telling us what he sees as he walks. Goldberger conflates tower and architect, telling (if not always showing) why Hearst is a building worthy of the skyscraper pantheon and Foster an architect to be classed with Sullivan and SOM. Each approach is equally valid and capable of adaptation. But each also builds on the history of the skyscraper, one that begins with Sullivan's words and work.

CHECKLIST

1. Know your history. To evaluate a skyscraper without a sense of the past
   will make choosing your superlative extremely difficult. Think about how
   Goldberger discusses history and makes Hearst seem ready to join the greats.

2. Consider your opening paragraphs in physical terms. What's the image you
   want to start with? Where is your reader positioned in relation to the building,
   literally or figuratively?

3. Choose your path. Will you walk the reader through the spaces inside to
   outside? Vice versa? Will you focus on the architect's career or his/her work?
   Be selective.

4. Return to Sullivan: is there something new here under the sun?

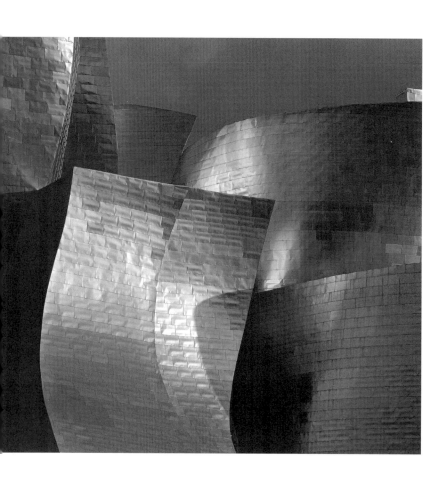

The Miracle in Bilbao

HERBERT MUSCHAMP

—————

New York Times Magazine, SEPTEMBER 7, 1997

PAGE 62

If you want to look into the heart of American art today, you are going to need a passport. You will have to pack your bags, leave the U.S.A. and find your way to Bilbao, a small, rusty city in the northeast corner of Spain. The trip is not convenient, and you should not expect to have much fun while you're there. This is Basque country. A region proudly, if not officially, independent from the rest of Spain, it is also bleakly free from Spanish sophistication. Oh, and by the way, you might get blown up. Basque country is not Bosnia. But it's not Disney World, either. History here has not been sanitized into a colorful spectacle for your viewing enjoyment. People are actually living history here, punctuated by periodic violence. Those who visit Bilbao, however, may come away thinking that art is not entirely remote from matters of life and death.

Bilbao has lately become a pilgrimage town. The word is out that miracles still occur, and that a major one has happened here. The city's new Guggenheim Museum, a satellite of the Solomon R. Guggenheim Foundation in New York, opens on October 19. But people have been flocking to Bilbao for nearly two years, just to watch the building's skeleton take shape. "Have you been to Bilbao?" In architectural circles, that question has acquired the status of a shibboleth. Have you seen the light? Have you seen the future? Does it work? Does it play?

Designed by Frank Gehry, the Bilbao Guggenheim is the most important building yet completed by the California architect. The miracle taking place here, however, is not Gehry's building, wondrous as it is. The miraculous occurrence is the extravagant optimism that enters into the outlook of those who have made the pilgrimage. What if American art has not, after all, played itself out to its last entropic wheeze? What if standards of cultural achievement have not irretrievably dissolved in the vast, tepid bath of relativity, telemarketing and manipulated public opinion? Has it even become possible, once again, to think about beauty as a form of truth?

Ring-a-ding-ding.

Frank Gehry, who is 68, has been an important figure in architecture since 1978, the year he completed the remodeling of his home in Santa Monica, California. An extensively overhauled version of a generic Dutch-roofed suburban house, the building employed an original vocabulary of crude industrial materials: chain-link fence, plywood, galvanized zinc, cinder block, exposed wood framing. These he arranged into a composition of lopsided cubes, exposed-stud walls and other unruly shapes. In the past five years, Gehry has completed such major buildings as the University of Toledo Center for the Visual Arts, the Frederick R. Weisman Museum in Minneapolis, the American Center in Paris, an office building in Prague. These projects not only represent an enlargement in architectural scale. They have also extended what seemed a purely private, idiosyncratic language into the larger dimension of public meaning.

Gehry's own house was a tour de force, but it was, after all, an architect's home. And a California architect's home, at that. Even 10 years ago, it wasn't uncommon to hear him described as "an artist"—a maker of sculptures rather than buildings—or "Looney Tunes." People still say such things, in fact. Yet the scale of the new buildings and their high-profile reception in the news media suggest that the architectural climate has changed. People now recognize not only that Gehry is an architect—one who can bring a major project like the Guggenheim in on time and budget—but that his work is able to arouse a broad range of meanings, associations and projections, not least in those who actively dislike it. The idea has gained wider acceptance that art and Looney-Tuneville actually speak to broad contemporary social and cultural norms. The real fruitcakes today may be those who persist in denying this.

Question for a Sunday afternoon: What is a masterpiece? (a) Gio Ponti said that the architect's task is to interpret a community to itself. (b) Iris Murdoch wrote, "Serious art is a continuous working of meaning in the light of the discovery of some truth." (c) Diana Vreeland once described *Vogue* magazine as "the myth of the next reality." (d) All of the above. Answer: (d) All of the above. Add up these ideas, and you won't be far from a working definition of the ideal America's greatest architects have long aspired to.

Another question: What is a community at the end of the twentieth century? A focus group, a concentration camp, a chat room on the Internet, an address book, a dance club, all those afflicted with a particular incurable disease, a gender, an age bracket, a waiting room, owners of silver BMW's, organized crime, everyone who swears by a particular brand of painkiller and a two-block stretch of Manhattan on any weekday at lunch hour.

Social fragmentation is one of the truths Frank Gehry has sought to explore in his work, not because he loves to see things fall apart but, on the contrary, because he seeks meaning in a culture that would otherwise dissolve all intelligence in a deluge of demographics. Truth No. 2: These differences are superficial. People need love and they need work. These are the places meaning comes from. Everything else is superfluous. Truth No. 3: Superfluous things are a hoot and a holler. Superficiality can be wonderful. The Myth of the Next Reality, a.k.a. Utopia, is that there is a place where differences and commonalities, unity and diversity, can be seen as the poles around which beauty revolves. The axis between these poles is called empathy.

That most divine of all human qualities—empathy—is the source of meaning in Frank Gehry's designs. His aim is not to found a school, not to create a style. Rather, he is possessed by the gaga nineteenth-century notion that by exercising their imaginations artists can inspire others to use their own.

From the airport, you approach Bilbao through a hilly landscape that grows gradually more civilized with the brutal mess of urban industry. The road cuts through a valley: Bilbao and its river, the Nervion, suddenly appear, spread out like a dreamscape, far beneath what you took to be a low point of the land. Gehry's building, too, flashes briefly into view, its curving walls of titanium steel glinting an unmistakable welcome. Then the taxi plunges into the city and the river disappears, the museum vanishes and you are swallowed up by the streets of an unremarkable town.

This entrance should be considered part of Gehry's design. Consider, by contrast, the approach to the Metropolitan Museum in New York, where the ceremonial way is paved via Fifth Avenue, a blocklong Beaux-Arts facade, a grand staircase. In Bilbao, the procession includes slag heaps, a decayed industrial riverfront, bridges, highway overpasses. The scene is neither sylvan nor classically urbane. But it strongly projects an image of the industrial power that drove the nineteenth-century city into being. That city is the wellspring of Frank Gehry's architecture. Often, he wears the costume of a working-class hero: blue shirts, windbreakers, baggy slacks. Some have taken this for affectation. It isn't. Gehry is a man deeply ingrained with appreciation for the industrial city as the place where 18th-century theories of modern democracy were put into messy practice, the place where wits, nerve, work, education and dreaming displaced ownership of land as the basis of the good life.

PAGE 63

Gehry was born too late to be a builder of that city. His career, rather, has corresponded to—indeed epitomizes—the transformation of the industrial metropolis into the post-industrial urban center, the place where tourism and cultural enterprise are now expected to fill the void left by the exportation of factory production to the third world. The standard remedy is: Send in the artists. Build a museum, a performing-arts center; change the zoning regulations so that industrial buildings can be converted to artists' lofts. The theory is that, in a post-industrial society, factory production will be supplanted by more creative work—that instead of blue-collar workers, the city will become home to "symbolic analysts," to use [American political economist and former Secretary of Labor] Robert Reich's phrase. In practice, production has given way to consumption: franchise outlets for cookies, ice cream, T-shirts; the invasion of the urban center by the ethos of the suburban mall. There are worse alternatives. Also better ones.

Bilbao, Spain's fourth-largest city, was once a shipbuilding town. The Bilbao Guggenheim is part of an ambitious plan to retool the city as an international center of culture and finance. Other projects, in addition to the

$100 million museum, include a new subway system with stations designed by Norman Foster and a new airport designed by Santiago Calatrava. The Guggenheim, which has been expanding its international operations since the appointment of Thomas Krens as director in 1988, reached an agreement to open the Bilbao branch six years ago. Two regional governments have underwritten the costs of constructing and operating it for at least 20 years. In exchange, the Guggenheim will provide use of its collection of modern and contemporary art, curatorial expertise and prestige.

Krens, who worked closely with Gehry on the museum's design, has been frequently maligned by those who resent his global aspirations, his wheeler-dealer ways. But let the bean counters count beans, the gum chewers chew gum. As the patron of projects by Gehry, Arata Isozaki, Gae Aulenti, Zaha Hadid and Hans Hollein, Krens has given architecture stronger support than any other American museum director in the past half-century.

In July, I go to meet Gehry in Bilbao for a preview of the museum. "Do you want to see the building?" he asks, when we meet at my hotel. What a card. We walk along the Calle de Iparraguirre, which frames a vista of the building's central rotunda. It strikes me that that street's visual clutter—parked cars, traffic signs, lampposts—magnify rather than distract from the building's impression. The museum looks like nothing else, but nonetheless looks at home. Even the dotted line painted down the middle of the street and the stripes of the pedestrian crosswalk at the corner look somehow Gehry-fied, an accidental version of the lines Renaissance artists used with such precision in architectural drawings to highlight the new laws of visual perspective.

The rotunda, rising 138 feet above street level, is wrapped with voluptuous curves of steel clad in titanium panels. The eye takes in this vista more as a mass of gathered light than as a proper building. The darkness of the narrow street turns the metal's brightness into a retinal explosion. But the light is soft. The metal seems to absorb light as well as reflect it, like the dull side of a piece of tinfoil. The expanses of titanium, partly discolored by weathering, are changed in appearance by clouds and the location of the sun. The metal folds mount higher toward the rotunda's center, like the leaves of an artichoke with clipped tips.

A pillbox of metal and glass protrudes at a slight tilt from the top of this steel blossom. As we walk toward the building, Gehry says that he now regrets this feature: "It looks like a pimple. But I guess it's O.K. for a face to have a pimple." On closer approach, a wing of more conventional dimensions slips into a view. It is boxy, as modern buildings were once supposed to be, and contains suites of classical galleries. The wing's rectangular contour serves as a foil, so to speak, for the foil. It is clad in honey-colored limestone. Light bounces back and forth between stone and metal as if within the facets of crystal embedded in rock.

A reverse grand staircase—funnel-shaped, it descends instead of rising—pours you into the building, leading you into the great spatial surprise of the museum's atrium. Even if you entered at ground level, the atrium would be a marvel. Contained spaces can seem immensely more vast than their containers—think of Frank Lloyd Wright's Guggenheim or New York's Grand Central Terminal. But because the staircase Gehry has designed draws you down a full story below ground level, the atrium pitches you into an enclosed version of the state of surreality that overtakes you on entering Bilbao. Pinch yourself, but don't wake up. It's better just to dream this.

The atrium offers a distilled concentration of the building's material vocabulary. Stone, glass, titanium, curves, straight lines, opacity, transparency, openness and enclosure are brought into sensuous conjunction. You may think, as you stand within this space, that the Tower of Babel story was a myth concocted by people who were afraid of diversity. Here you see that many languages can not only coexist but also babble around within a broad and vibrant vista of the world.

Galleries stretch out from the atrium in a variety of shapes and sizes. Two wings contain classically rectangular, if overscaled, galleries that open off one another in the traditional linear enfilade. Rubens's gigantic allegorical paintings of Marie de' Medici, one of the Louvre's finest treasures, would look fabulous here. The symmetrical form of the galleries is partly masked by the exterior's metal whorls, and also by the petal shapes of the galleries clustered round them. By now, you get the point that something is being said here on behalf of irregularity. Hurtling off in a third direction, parallel to the riverfront, is the most dramatic of the galleries, a 433-foot-long tube of space: a tunnel or internal boulevard. Gehry calls it "the boat." As you proceed along it, there are shifts in scale and contour, as there might be on a city street. The ceiling, supported by giant, white trusses, drops in a swift decline from an outlandishly high 85 feet to less than half that. The walls contract; the acoustics change.

The show doesn't end here. It continues outside, where the exit to the riverfront is even more ceremonially grand than the building's entrance. A metal canopy, held aloft by a single slender column, seems to billow in the breeze 92 feet above the ground, and the entire riverfront facade looks windswept. Toward the right, a city bridge slips over a corner of the building, the roadway forking into two overpasses as it makes contact. Then, on the bridge's far side, the building flares up into a pair of steel towers, their arcs echoing, in vertical form, the fork in the road.

The towers are clad on three sides only, revealing the metal framework within. Though containing no usable spaces, they are not functionless. They enable the museum to be seen along the river and from the city's downtown. Like the Twin Towers in New York, they are symbols of themselves. And they are also emblematic of Gehry's intention to merge with urban infrastructure. In the past, Gehry has often used building skins as wrappers, surfaces that part to reveal the volume within. Here, he has used three-dimensional forms to wrap his arms around a city.

At the time of my visit, only one artwork had been installed, Richard Serra's "Snake." Perhaps it is not possible to evaluate the building without considering the question of how well it functions as a showcase for art. It may be, however, that one of this building's major functions is to live that question

PAGE 65

through. Over time, people will judge how well or how badly the museum displays individual works of art. But these judgments may well be shaped by the increasing awareness that art resides only partly within individual art-works. It also lives in the spirit of risk and experimentation that works of art help sustain. This awareness is a central characteristic of the post-industrial city, as well as a theme of contemporary art. Art has spilled out of its classical containers into performance, the media, fashion and other ephemeral forms of expression. By the same token, at least since the advent of conceptual art, the task for many artists has been not only to create objects but also to escape their confining dimensions.

The Bilbao Guggenheim is an object, of course, however skillfully Gehry has intertwined the museum with the city around it. Still, inside and out, it's a spectacular embodiment of the tension between objects and the world beyond them. Within these far-from-neutral galleries, artworks will inevitably be drawn into complex relationships with the architecture and with one another. Outside, the design overflows any ordinary conception of what a museum, or any building, should resemble. Like the Basque region, this building is a place of contested borders.

Gehry says that like many young architects, he started out wanting to change the world. He was concerned with city planning, social justice, a more equitable environment. Yet he has managed to effect change on a scale few architects achieve.

In Los Angeles in 1983, Gehry took a service station for municipal vehicles and converted it into the Temporary Contemporary museum, a building that declared an end to the city's sense of cultural inferiority far more effectively than Arata Isozaki's permanent Museum of Contemporary Art. The Temporary's shrewd and gritty informality told Los Angelenos that an architectural intelligence of unequaled stature was one of their own.

Gehry's impact has been on consciousness, that is to say, not just particular parcels of land. And in the post-industrial city, it may no longer be possible to divorce consciousness from material reality. What was once the radical outlook of Surrealism has become part of the logic of everyday life. Ideas, images and illusions now occupy the places once held by sweaters, ball bearings and vacuum tubes.

Several weeks ago, when I was visiting Los Angeles, Gehry said, "You know, I wasn't supposed to be this." Meaning, I suppose, this big honcho. Or this big Looney Tune. I didn't press him to say how he used to think his life would turn out. I didn't want to force him to be falsely modest, or even genuinely so. But it must be scary to find people looking at you and writing about you as a person who has changed an art form and in the process is changing a culture. I imagine that sometimes Gehry must feel like the movie director Marcello Mastroianni plays in Fellini's "8," when, during the news conference scene, he tries to crawl under the table to get away as one of the reporters cackles with glee: "He has nothing to say! Nothing to say!"

In one sense, in fact, Gehry does have nothing to say. His language is architecture, not words. Though Gehry actually writes with beautiful clarity and his lectures have become extraordinary pieces of stand-up humor, he distrusts words. He lives on the opposite side of the world from architects like Peter Eisenman who feel that they cannot proceed safely into the world unless armored with academic jargon.

The first time I visited Gehry's Santa Monica office, I had to fight off a feeling of awkwardness, because he was so taciturn. Basically, he just guided me around, pausing here and there to point out and just barely identify a model for a new project or a sample of materials. Since I was there to learn, I took Gehry's silence as part of the lesson. I sensed he felt that words have the power to limit, and therefore to exclude. People can make their own pictures.

Gehry sometimes does put labels on buildings, but usually these are like jokes or pet names. (In Prague, there's "Fred and Ginger.") Rarely, he will include a form that's explicitly metaphoric: in Paris, there's a series of glass panels, jutting out at different angles, that are meant to be a symbol of the openness of American culture and of France's receptivity to the United States. More typically, a figurative element will turn up transformed into an abstraction. Once I mentioned to Gehry that part of his design for the Walt Disney Concert Hall in Los Angeles reminded me of the scalloped side of a bass viol. He wasn't dismayed that the source of an abstract shape had been recognized. He said, "You know, I have been looking at that!"

Fools give you reasons. Wise men never try. An architecture critic has no choice but to be foolish on this occasion, however. If a critic wants to say that the Bilbao Guggenheim is, in effect, a Lourdes for a crippled culture, then some kind of case must be made.

The Bilbao Guggenheim is approached through time as well as space: to get there, the visitor passes through history and geography both. This building's design and construction have coincided with the waning of a period when American architecture spectacularly lost its way.

Post-modernism, "with its sad air of the parade's gone by," in [*New Yorker* dance critic (1973–1998)] Arlene Croce's choice phrase, started out as a constructive movement. In the mid-1960's, a few architects set out to educate themselves about the history of an art form that a Bauhaus-influenced education had plowed under. Gifted architects like Robert Venturi, Aldo Rossi and Charles Moore used these ideas to free themselves from the strangulating orthodoxies of the modern movement. This period lasted for 10 years. By the mid-1980's, the movement had deteriorated into a career strategy for reactionaries, opportunists and their deeply uncultivated promoters. These people had spent, maybe, a summer vacation in Europe and somehow arrived at the belief that this experience entitled them to be spokesmodels for the Great Western Tradition. Even without the help of the Disney company, architecture plummeted into the realm of the packaged tour.

Post-modernism gained architects esthetic freedom. Few made good use of it. Despite intermittent creative flashes, the movement overall resembled a shelf of Harlequin romance novels pretentiously mislabeled as literature. I think of the past 20 years as the Franziska Schankowska period of American architecture, in honor of the Polish factory worker who jumped into a Berlin canal and resurfaced moments later as the Grand Duchess Anastasia.

Like Schankowska, many post-modernists were inspired dreamers and schemers, but their movement bore no more relation to history than Schankowska did to the Romanovs. Instead, it pandered to people's fear of history, holding out the delusion that they could step out of their own life and times.

One reason people have descended on Bilbao with such hope is that with this building, American architecture has jumped back into the present with a splash. This antique art form has made it. It has come through. And so has the consensus of informed opinion that once made it possible to say, This is better than that.

It can take awhile for an event to work its way into consciousness. After my first visit to the building, I went back to the hotel to write notes. It was early evening and starting to rain. I took a break to look out the window and saw a woman standing alone outside a bar across the street. She was

PAGE 66

wearing a long, white dress with matching white pumps, and she carried a pearlescent handbag. Was her date late? Had she been stood up?

PAGE 66
When I looked back a bit later, she was gone. And I asked myself, Why can't a building capture a moment like that? Then I realized that the reason I'd had that thought was that I'd just come from such a building. And that the building I'd just come from was the reincarnation of Marilyn Monroe.

There's a scene in "The Misfits" in which she goes out to Eli Wallach's unfinished house in the Nevada desert to try the house, the desert and her future on for size. "I can go in and I can come out—I can go in and I can come out," Monroe cries with delight, after some cinder blocks were put down where the front step is supposed to be. Wallach points to the unadorned balloon frame: "This was gonna be another bedroom." Monroe says wistfully, "It's even nice this way." What twins the actress and the building in my memory is that both of them stand for an American style of freedom. That style is voluptuous, emotional, intuitive and exhibitionist. It is mobile, fluid, material, mercurial, fearless, radiant and as fragile as a newborn child. It can't resist doing a dance with all the voices that say "No." It wants to take up a lot of space. And when the impulse strikes, it likes to let its dress fly up in the air.

What was Monroe's secret for looking sexy on film? Maybe she took her acting teacher's advice and thought about Frank Sinatra and a Coke. What does Frank Gehry think about when he is coaxing these mercurial images out of his mind? He could be thinking about a fish. In interviews, the architect has said that as a child his schoolmates called him "Fish." It seems that his grandmother used to prepare gefilte fish in the bathtub of the apartment where he grew up and that the scent clung to his skin. True or not, the fish has been a recurring image in Gehry's work for many years. He has designed lamps, restaurants, even bus stops in the form of fish. The panels of metal and stone applied to the surface of the Guggenheim adhere to the overlapping pattern of scales.

PAGE 67
Gehry and Monroe never met. But for a period of time they reclined on the same couch; consulted the same analyst, anyhow. Even without knowing that, you recognize that Bilbao is a sanctuary of free association. It's a bird, it's a plane, it's Superman. It's a ship, an artichoke, the miracle of the rose. A first glimpse of the building tells you that the second glimpse is going

to be different from the first. A second glimpse tells you that a third is going to be different still. If there is an order to this architecture, it is not one that can be predicted from one or two visual slices of its precisely calculated free-form geometry. But the building's spirit of freedom is hard to miss.

PAGE 67

You can go in, and you can come out. The interplay between in and out has been a recurring theme of architecture for the past century. The open floor plan of Frank Lloyd Wright. The primary colors and forms of Theo van Doesburg. The glass-curtain walls of Ludwig Mies van der Rohe. Twentieth-century architecture has unfolded as a series of variations on the relationship between the interior and exterior of buildings, bodies, minds—between public and private realms. Gehry extends this tradition into an era when communications technology is further shifting the boundaries between public and private space, and when an awareness of psychology has permeated and transformed the dynamics of public and private life. But his means of extending that tradition are not the same as those of the classical modernists. Instead of trying to further reduce architectural form to the bare minimum, he has gone deeper into the psychological space where images are formed and further out into the city that helps to shape them.

I realized on that first visit to Gehry's office that his designs offer few clues to the inner recesses of the architect's mind. Rather, they are an invitation for viewers to explore their own. His main preoccupation is with subtly adjusting the relationships among the forms he employs. Mine is to learn why, upon leaving his Guggenheim, a 49-year-old architecture critic might suddenly find himself speaking in the voice of Marilyn Monroe. Her presence in Bilbao is totally my projection. Gehry's delight in arousing such responses, however, is genuine.

Titanium is tough. But it's a piece of Kleenex compared with the mind of an introvert who has learned to function in extroverted ways. Isn't this the great lesson of all art museums? Even if you only think of them as excellent places to cruise, you get the basic idea. For an hour or so, you get to share the same space with a group of strangers. As you can see for yourself from the stuff on the walls, the possibilities are endless.

PAGE 67

That is not the kind of contact that architecture ordinarily encourages. This is not a field in which introverts easily flourish. But occasionally power and imagination join hands; the Guggenheim Museum effected such a union half a century ago when it hired Frank Lloyd Wright to design its building on Fifth Avenue. It has done so once again with its new building in Bilbao.

It's not so tough for painters or sculptors to project empathy into the world. That's what the public expects from artists, after all. Ah, yes, artists, such sensitive souls, so creative and tragic. And now it's Sunday. We will go to a museum and peer into their troubled souls. And then have brunch. Bloody Mary or mimosa? But when empathy enters into architecture, a milestone has been reached. An art form that has long depended upon appeals to external authority—history, science, context, tradition, religion, philosophy or style— has at last come to the realization that nobody cares about that sort of thing anymore. Architecture has stepped off her pedestal. She's waiting for her date outside a bar on a rainy early evening in Bilbao, Spain.

The Bilbao Guggenheim is cause for collective pride. If one lesson can be salvaged from the painted desert in which American architecture has been stranded in recent years, it is this: When a culture lets itself settle for anything less than great, there's no telling how low it will sink. Nor is it easy to recognize the moment when the rot sets in. Architecture, no less than politics, is an art of the possible. The field has almost infinite tolerance for those who want to rob space of decency and meaning.

Here's the saving grace. We know what it's like to feel fully alive. The feeling may not happen often, but when it does, we're there. It can happen at the movies, watching baseball, while dancing, in love, at the beach, on a street, in the company of others or in perfect solitude. However long it lasts, it's an undeniable fact. It's not a theory, not a yearning for the unattainable. It's a real reason to scream. Lose composure. Throw hats into the air. It's a victory for all when any one of us finds a path into freedom, as Frank Gehry has this year in Bilbao, and beyond.

CHAPTER 2

WHAT SHOULD A MUSEUM BE?

If towers are growing ever taller, becoming ever greener and ever more evocative as expressions of architectural or political might, museums are growing ever weirder, one-upping each other with spiky or spongy shapes, outrageous transparency or luxurious amenities. The debate over the box versus the blob—really an argument about the higher purpose of a museum, the art or the architecture—has been going on since the opening of Frank Lloyd Wright's spiral Guggenheim in 1959.

On one side, the blob: a building of radical appearance, typically by a famous architect, whose structure alone attracts an audience and creates an identity for whatever institution it houses. The institution's collection (or orchestra—they can also be concert halls) may or may not be well served. It can look like and be made of almost anything. Exemplary projects include Daniel Libeskind's 2006 expansion of the Denver Art Museum, Zaha Hadid's 2009 MAXXI in Rome, and Frank Gehry's 1997 Guggenheim Bilbao. On the other side, the box: rectilinear and monochromatic, with glass walls or elaborate overhead daylighting systems, galleries meaningless without art. To paraphrase practitioner Yoshio Taniguchi, architect of the Museum of Modern Art's 2004 expansion, it is an architecture intended to disappear. Exemplary projects include almost all of Renzo Piano's museums and expansions (from the 1987 Menil Collection in Houston through his 2009 wing for the Art Institute of Chicago), Tadao Ando's 2001 Pulitzer Foundation in St. Louis and 2002 Modern Art Museum of Fort Worth, and SANAA's 2007 New Museum in Manhattan.

In 1959 the rivals were slightly different. Wright's Guggenheim ended
the equivalence of the Beaux-Arts block—with its wide stairs, multistory columns,
and broad flanks—with the idea of a museum. But it did not replace that model,
promulgated by McKim, Mead & White, Carrère & Hastings, and other Gilded Age
firms, with something equally universal. In the 1950s and 1960s, architects of every
modernist stripe designed new museums and additions to old structures for cities
interested in revitalizing their cultural centers and making room for contemporary
art. In Ada Louise Huxtable's 1960 essay "What Should a Museum Be?," she pointed
to Mies van der Rohe's Houston Museum of Fine Arts, Edward Durell Stone's
drawings for Huntington Hartford's Gallery of Modern Art at 2 Columbus Circle
(now the Museum of Arts & Design) in New York, and a quartet of rather unexciting
Philip Johnson museum projects as exemplars of the museum boom then underway.
The 1960s would bring Marcel Breuer's Whitney Museum in Manhattan, SOM's
Albright-Knox Art Gallery in Buffalo and Hirshhorn Museum in Washington, Louis
Kahn's Kimbell Museum in Fort Worth, and many, many more. About these projects
Huxtable writes, "The new buildings are startling, even shocking in appearance.
They follow no set architectural formula; each designer offers his own idea of how
to house the museum's updated functions. The temptation to turn a structure into a
personal statement occasionally has proved irresistible."

The museum boom in the United States that Huxtable chronicles closely
mirrors one experienced internationally in the 1990s and 2000s, one that also upset
established modern notions of how a museum should look and act. In a nice piece of
parallelism, the building that kicked off the later boom is also a Guggenheim, Gehry's
museum in Bilbao. "The Miracle in Bilbao," a piece of criticism published on
September 7, 1997 in the *New York Times Magazine*, is as controversial for its literary
form as for the forms it describes, and in it Herbert Muschamp offers a highly
personal, idiosyncratic answer to Huxtable's question.

Muschamp's review is the centerpiece of this chapter, as it is exemplary of
his experiential and emotional *approach* to architecture criticism and of its elasticity
as a form. In the first chapter, the three critics stuck close to the skyscraper as a type,
taking their comparisons from history, engineering, and the city itself. Muschamp, in
contrast, takes his comparisons from music, comic books, movies, sociology, spinning

a cloud of cultural reference around the building and architect in question. Unlike the reviews in the first chapter, Muschamp's should not be taken as a model of *theme*, *approach*, and *organization* as a whole (though it is instructive in parts) but rather as an example of criticism taken to the limit and conducted with maximum imagination.

What you should get from this chapter is first, that there is an idea of the method to Muschamp's madness. In his review, myriad approaches to the subject of museum surface within a bewildering flurry of overlapping references. Part of Muschamp's project is to expand the role of the museum (and hence the role of architecture) to that of urban, even global, player, and this requires travels far from the galleries. In Huxtable's essay "What Should a Museum Be?," she created an opposition between showcasing art or architecture. Muschamp does not talk about the picture-hanging system or the lighting. He barely talks about the art. Instead, he talks about the museum's mood and all the things one does in a museum besides look at art. Muschamp also offers multiple suggestions about what other media have to say about architecture.

What a museum should be is a bigger question now than it was in 1960. In order to engage with the museum as a critic, you have to understand the museum both as an interior, focused on the display of its collection, and as an exterior that is part of an urban ensemble, a development strategy, and possibly a city's transformation to global player. If it takes a Superman reference to make that point, Muschamp is game.

Muschamp, the *New York Times* architecture critic from 1992 to 2004, was a deeply polarizing figure. He took over the job from Paul Goldberger, who was seen as a supporter of big-name architects and big-name developers, an explainer, a historian, but not a writer of particular style or emotion. Muschamp, by contrast, was a writer of flamboyant style and sometimes excessive emotion. The mood of a building might be characterized with slang, music lyrics (retro, not hip-hop), Romantic poetry, or film clips. The journey from the entrance to the gallery, up into the crown, and back out to the plaza could take a paragraph or the entire review, so studded was his prose with digression and references. In "A Queens Factory Is Born Again, as a Church," a 1999 review of the New York Presbyterian Church in Queens, an early example of blobitecture—by young turks Doug Garofalo, Greg Lynn, and Michael McInturf—Muschamp writes, of computer modeling: "Space becomes as plastic as Silly Putty. It can be pinched, rotated, kneaded, stretched, cut into sections, shattered and left to ooze....For the church, [Lynn] and his partners have invented a form they call Nestor....Imagine it as the hollow cavity of a Jurassic fossil."

It is hard to imagine the critics of the previous generation managing the leap from child's plaything to sculpting advanced digital design and then to dinosaurs, but Muschamp makes it flow. There's a picture in his head of the building, and he is using any means necessary to communicate that to his reader.

At first Muschamp seemed an odd fit for the *Times*. He knew it too, and wrote of his early insecurity in an essay titled "Critical Reflections," which appeared in the May 1995 *ArtForum*:

> The job, in other words, is sacred, and it can be inhibiting to inhabit something sacred. One fears soiling it, fears thinking of it too much as an "it," an existing model to which, swayed by the eminence of the institution, one feels obligated to tailor one's ideas....
>
> ...At one point before I was hired, I asked Max [Frankel, the executive editor at the time] if I could occasionally write for other publications. Max agreed, then added, "But if you have something to say, and you don't say it here, you're crazy."
>
> This was the best thing he could have said. Up to that point, I'd been allowing myself to fear that the job wasn't really about whether or not I had anything to say, it was about trying to figure out what an institution like the *Times* "ought" to say. By his assumption that what I would say in the column was what *I* had to say, though, Max was telling me to be myself.

What Muschamp had to say and the way he wanted to say it are nowhere in better evidence than his review of Guggenheim Bilbao. "The Miracle in Bilbao" was widely read, reaching a far larger audience than typical for architecture criticism. And it established Gehry as the architect for the new century. "The Bilbao Effect," the title of an article by architectural historian and current *Slate* architecture critic Witold Rybcynski in the *Atlantic* in September 2002, came to signify the idea that a city could put itself on the map via a piece of signature architecture. The Bilbao effect was in the future as Muschamp was writing, but his opening paragraphs anticipate the globalization of architectural stars and architectural style. The future can happen anywhere, as can American art: "If you want to look into the heart of American art today, you are going to need a passport. You will have to pack your bags, leave the U.S.A. and find your way to Bilbao, a small, rusty city in the northeast corner of Spain."

Rather than being published in the Arts & Leisure section, as Muschamp's reviews typically were, this was a *New York Times Magazine* cover story. The cover image showed the billowing forms of Gehry's titanium-clad museum tightly squeezed between the gray stone facades of a traditional Bilbao street. It looks—to attempt a Muschampian association—like the skirts of a queen's dress, suggesting that the so-called miracle is the appearance of royalty in Basque country.

It is with that sense of wonder that Muschamp begins his review, calling upon you, the reader, to make the trip. The detachment of critics like Mumford and Huxtable is nowhere in evidence. Muschamp is going to pull. He uses the second person, rare in criticism, to advance his sense of urgency. (A shibboleth, by the way, is the jargon of the in-crowd. If you haven't seen the building, he suggests, you aren't going to be able to enter the global cultural conversation.) Muschamp uses the opening paragraphs of his review to establish the importance of Gehry's building beyond architecture. His word choices create a network of associations within a broad public realm: pilgrimage with religion, Disney World with tourism, Bosnia with geopolitics, work and play with daily life. This review is intended to carve a larger space for architecture in the world, merging the ambitions of the architect with the ambitions of the critic.

But what about the architecture? The reviews by Huxtable and Mumford previously discussed mostly describe buildings—the building under consideration and its neighbors. Even Goldberger's review of the Hearst Tower, heavy as it is on personality and action verbs, spends time on description. One might wonder, as his critics often did, when Muschamp is going to get to the building itself.

In this piece, it takes a while, not least because Muschamp begins his promenade architecturale—a term, coined by Le Corbusier, for the journey through a building as mapped by its architect—way back at the airport. This approach is distinctly different from that taken in most architecture reviews, in which the building can be part of an appraisal of the neighborhood or is compared to its urban contemporaries, but the focus is still relatively tight. Rather than starting at the base of a flight of neoclassical steps (as Muschamp does during his mention of the Metropolitan Museum), Muschamp begins at the airport, a nod to the tourism he knows the museum will attract. The trip with Muschamp takes you past the detritus of twentieth-century industrial civilization, as it is industry—and its attendant effect of opening up economies, markets, and opportunities for all—that Muschamp sees as the antecedent to Gehry's design. Including the drive from the airport gives the museum a history and a grounding it might otherwise lack.

In recent years, critics have metaphorically parachuted in to see the work of Gehry and his fellow architects around the world—to Beijing, Dubai, Singapore, and Rome. This can lead to an impoverishing lack of context: how can you talk about a building's role in the city, even on its block, if you come, look, leave? Muschamp suggests a different approach for the critic and visitor, and a consideration of the museum as part of a larger trip. All of Huxtable's inquiries concerned the envelope of the museum itself. Muschamp sees and describes the impact of Gehry's sculptural forms from much farther away: "The scene is neither sylvan nor classically urbane. But it strongly projects an image of the industrial power that drove the 19th-century city into being. That city is the wellspring of Frank Gehry's architecture. Often, he wears the costume of a working-class hero: blue shirts, windbreakers, baggy slacks. Some have taken this for affectation. It isn't."

The shift from the building to the man is another classic Muschamp maneuver. Like Goldberger, who conflates the energy of the Hearst Tower with that of its architect, Norman Foster, Muschamp reads the Guggenheim Bilbao through Gehry's biography—wardrobe and all. Muschamp had done this before, most famously in a long appraisal of the architectural legacy of Donald Trump, "Trump, His Gilded Taste, and Me" (also headlined, "Architecture as Personality"), published in the *Times* on December 19, 1999:

> To me, [Trump's] buildings don't quite register as architecture. They look
> to me like signs of money, status, power. These signs are fascinating in
> their own right, as are diamonds, furs, yachts, and other tokens of the
> deluxe life enjoyed in Marbella, St. Bart's, and other playgrounds of the
> rich. To Mr. Trump, quality means luxury details—fine marble, imported
> wood, sparkling fixtures—and fast-track construction. To me, it means
> risk-taking ideas, original perceptions, spirit of place and time, and
> self-construction—the same qualities Mr. Trump projects in his public
> persona, in fact.

There is a certain in-crowd sensibility to this emphasis on personality, and at times in the Bilbao review, Muschamp makes his long-standing friendship with Gehry explicit. He makes no pretense of objectivity. Muschamp suggests that he knows better how to read the building because he knows the architect, and he's letting us in on the secret.

He classes Gehry with artists, rather than the consumers, though Gehry, post-Bilbao, has clearly become a brand name (a "designer" of jewelry for Tiffany & Co., among other ventures). Cultural production, within transforming cities, typically occurred when artists moved into former factories and started making new work in areas left for dead. Their renovations eventually brought people with money around to create retail spaces, condominiums, and the kind of new development that drives real-estate prices too high for the artists to stay. At Bilbao, Muschamp casts Gehry as one of those pioneers and the museum as an incubator of art rather than its final resting place. He argues that this museum is dynamic rather than historic due to its architectural style as well as Gehry's liberal, antibourgeois political background. Instead of a repository of artistic treasures, it is a treasure in itself—and a generator of future art.

This redefinition of the museum's role allows Muschamp to sidestep part of Huxtable's question: his ideal museum doesn't have to be a good place to display art. In fact, when Huxtable herself reviewed the Guggenheim Bilbao, she set aside her previous reservations and embraced the change. The title of her review? "Art and Architecture as One":

The collaboration between director and architect on this building has been unique. Most museum directors opt for negative, or "recessive," space; they favor neutrality as an aid to installation. Mr. Krens encouraged Mr. Gehry to take his place with the other artists; he encouraged the spatial drama of the atrium, the startling shapes and dimensions of the new galleries....Moreover, Mr. Krens is convinced that the constantly increasing size of much contemporary art makes it virtually impossible to exhibit in normal surroundings, and that to do so diminishes its impact and meaning.

It is a new world, for art and for the museum, and Huxtable has changed her criteria, accepting, by quoting without comment, Guggenheim director Thomas Krens's idea that the architecture needs to join art in scale and ambition. She and Muschamp are, somewhat unexpectedly, in agreement. Many continue to question whether a large, expensive building, however radical, can transform a city's economy without relying on the very tourism Muschamp dismisses. Muschamp wants the Guggenheim Bilbao to spawn a new generation of Basque artists, future Gehrys, equally intoxicated by the ruins. But there has been little evidence of a Bilbao renaissance—except for more urban architecture by international figures.

What should be learned from Muschamp's critical approach is how other disciplines can be included in architectural criticism. He displays a deep knowledge of urban history and cultural development, simultaneously commenting on the roots of the Industrial Revolution and ideas about the role of artists in real-estate development later encapsulated in urban theorist Richard Florida's *The Rise of the Creative Class* (2002). He does not confine himself to talking about the building, its materials, and its ability to display art. He talks about it as part of a much bigger picture, and the motifs of that picture continue to multiply as he heads toward conclusion.

It is only at approximately halfway through his five-thousand-word review that he proceeds with building description, moving from outside to inside and back again, noting: "At the time of my visit, only one artwork had been installed, Richard Serra's 'Snake.'" But Muschamp never evaluates how the Corten-steel Serra looks in the long gallery specifically designed to hold it. He pauses by the sculpture only to expand on the idea of art as an urban actor. The artifact (as represented by the Serra) isn't important to him; what is important is the act of making, the return of production to Bilbao. To Muschamp the museum isn't a repository but a performance space.

In "What Should a Museum Be?," Huxtable acknowledges the social purpose of the museum: "The building should be handsome enough to be a recognizable landmark, important and interesting enough to attract visitors; a museum without people is no museum at all." Muschamp takes the museums-are-for-people idea further. To him the museum is art and performance, still and movie, and we are all both viewers and parts of the film. We see this in the three sections of the review—which I am going to call Marilyn, Superman, and brunch—in which Muschamp articulates his flights of fancy and fantasy. In a typical newspaper review, he might allow himself only a reference to a poet or actor of relevance to the architectural experience. Here he lets us in on the many teeming associations in his brain and takes the idea of architectural criticism to its limit.

He writes, "The building I'd just come from was the reincarnation of Marilyn Monroe." The Guggenheim Bilbao *is* Marilyn Monroe? At first the brain does not compute. But try to see what Muschamp is getting at. After all, from the first paragraph, he described the museum as *American* art. Marilyn was as equally American, equally a work of art. She embodied star quality, as the museum does. She was voluptuous, as the museum is. She was attention getting—that skirt over the grate was no accident—as the museum is. Throughout the review he has been trying to make the museum into an actor, a player on various world stages of culture and economic development and tourism. He wants it to move as, he argues, art today moves from airport to downtown to river, from grungy former factory to fancy condominium to museum. He has to find a figure to embody the Guggenheim's appeal, and he finds it in Marilyn.

The lesson for the writer is to let the imagination run wild, even if you end up editing out any overly zealous material. The critic can use any means necessary to describe what s/he sees, and sometimes turning to a pop image or a personality may be the easiest, and most effective, path. Architecture is not hermetic.

Metaphor and association outside the world of buildings can help let others in on what we feel when we are in architecture. A critic only has words, and the world of extra-visual association offers additional colors to the palette. That's why Gehry and Muschamp make such a perfect couple. Gehry, atypical of contemporary architects, courts metaphor and association. Muschamp sees fish and roses and film stars: "Bilbao is a sanctuary of free association. It's a bird, it's a plane, it's Superman. It's a ship, an artichoke, the miracle of the rose." (You might see something else.) As a critic, Muschamp seizes that freedom and becomes the voice of the building, dispensing with distance and much of the review form discussed in chapter 1. But he doesn't get rid of all of it: there is structure beneath the billowing, associative skin.

When walking through a building, don't ignore the pictures or poems or sounds that come into your head. Take notes on what you see, but also be attuned to subconscious insight, points of attraction, ideas of connection.

Long before the advent of the iPhone, now ubiquitous in museums as guided apps and cameras, and Twitter, which people use to announce their presence in front of a work of art, Muschamp uses the idea of social experience to form the conclusion to his fantastic journey to Bilbao. Muschamp was one of the first critics to acknowledge (without negative judgment) the turn museums had taken to mimic the mall, with food courts and shopping as part of the experience.

By speaking directly to *you*, his reader, he's been trying to make the trip social from the start. He's been trying to prove that the museum has a role much bigger than as art container, reattaching abandoned neighborhoods to their cities. He's been trying to turn the museum into a person, like Marilyn, with whom we all dream of drinking a cocktail. What's his ultimate point? Maybe that the Guggenheim Bilbao proves museums can be fun—with or without the art, "even if you only think of them as excellent places to cruise."

Muschamp starts and ends with you. He's led you by the hand to Bilbao on the taxi ride from the airport, through the museum, and back to the hotel. He's filled your mind with associations, and now together you and he sit by the window, catching a breath of fresh air. Marilyn appears, and you go downstairs to meet her. She's waiting for you.

For Muschamp approach is key. He puts empathy, not function or organization, first in his criteria to make the argument for architecture as art. Museums are his best subject because they have constantly provoked questions about the role of architecture: Should it showcase or compete? Is the client the director, the artist, or the public? Should it provoke or entomb? And which comes first: gallery, gift shop, or cafe? The turn-of-the-twentieth-century Beaux-Arts buildings to which Huxtable referred reified the objects within them, sealing them off from the contemporary scene by declaring their importance in history. The new museums have a more fluid relationship to contemporary art and artists and to the act of making. Bilbao was a gesture equivalent to artists colonizing abandoned industrial spaces; the building's design took the museum conventions out of the museum and made the audience *feel* something again.

If chapter 1 suggested a variety of replicable forms for the architecture review, then in a sense Muschamp's review undermines those forms. However, even in his expansive and discursive text, we can locate the three elements of critique: theme, in his opening, second-person paragraph, which makes it clear that a trip to Bilbao is much more than a visit to a building (other themes appear in turn, such as the museum as urban savior and the museum as social connector); approach, in his welter of associated images, anecdotes, and references, all engineered to communicate the thrill of that trip; and (if you break it into smaller parts) organization, in his own version of a walk-through like Mumford, a city visit like Huxtable, and an association of architect and building like Goldberger—he just does all three.

Muschamp doesn't just talk about Marilyn and the museum; rather, he uses the anecdote involving Monroe to try to draw the reader into criticism in a more emotional way. His anecdote, like his description of that Queens church using Silly Putty and Jurassic fossils, is another way of connecting.

CHECKLIST

1. "A Miracle in Bilbao" suggests an exercise in freeing the mind for similar associative descriptors. Pick a building, preferably a museum. Write down ten things it makes you think of, none of them related to architecture. What superhero would it be? Does it have a theme song? What role could it play in the plot of a romantic comedy? Are its overtones poetic, scientific, commercial, environmental?

2. Now come back down to earth. Consider the museum's effect on its surroundings at different scales. Is the building part of a larger development plan? Is it the beginning or the end of that plan? Are there buildings of similar ambition (or buildings at all) nearby, or is it an orphan? How might the building play a role—a personality like Donald Trump—in your urban narrative?

3. Go inside. What is the relationship of inside to outside? Of container to contents? Who is the building for? What does the architecture make most important: the building, the collection, the gift shop, the cafe?

4. To paraphrase Huxtable: What is this particular museum's strength and style? Identify that quality, and then use your version of Muschamp's free associations to communicate those strengths to the reader. Make them feel like they have made the pilgrimage too.

Save the Whitney

MICHAEL SORKIN

Village Voice, JUNE 25, 1985

History seems poised to take its revenge on poor Marcel Breuer. The late architect, you may recall, was justly lambasted some years ago for designing a scheme to place an office tower on the roof of Grand Central Station. Opposition to that venture was the Agincourt of local preservationism, a victory after which the climate changed decisively. Now, the Whitney Museum, in apparent tit for Breuer's historic tat, proposes to expand itself by building on top of his great gray granite original an architectural affront of such magnitude that the only conceivable explanation is whimsical redress of the dead man's nearly forgotten gaffe. Poetic justice, however, will be symmetrically served only if the current scheme meets the fate of the former.

The Breuer Whitney is a masterpiece. With Edward Durrell Stone's original Museum of Modem Art and Frank Lloyd Wright's Guggenheim Museum, it completes a trinity of marvelous museums, a virtual recapitulation of the modern movement. All three of these institutions have lately felt the need to expand and all have been imperiled. At MOMA, the damage is already done: the original building has been reduced to its facade, its elevation hanging like a modernist painting on a gallery wall. Plans for the Guggenheim have not been revealed in detailed form. Perhaps the threatened intrusion will be held at bay by the totemic power of Wright's original, the master of hubris hexing attempts at effacement from beyond the grave.

At the Whitney, there's no doubt. The violence offered by Michael Graves's proposed expansion is almost unbelievable. Adding to a masterpiece is always difficult, calling for discipline, sensitivity, restraint. Above all, though,

PAGE 82

it calls for respect. The Graves addition isn't simply disrespectful, it's hostile, an assault on virtually everything that makes the Breuer original particular. It's a petulant, Oedipal piece of work, an attack on a modernist father by an upstart, intolerant child, blind or callow perhaps, but murderous. Yet for this the blame is not entirely the architect's. Society asked him to do it. Graves, after all, is a designer with an idiom and could scarcely be expected to throttle his own voice at a moment of tremendous expansion in his career. Graves was simply a wrong choice. The degree of the error is what startles—somebody with influence must really have hated the Breuer building.

PAGE 82

The strength of the Whitney's architecture is not simply its singularity but its refined embodiment of the modernist spirit. Breuer may be presently out of vogue, but he's indisputably one of the tops. A member of the core cadre at the Bauhaus, Breuer wound up in the U.S. after the school was shut down by the Nazis. Like the furniture for which he's so universally renowned, his architecture is shapely, strong, and frank. It shows the craftsperson's love of construction and materials, attentive always to an idea of integrity that modernism elevated to an ethic. For Breuer, pouring concrete and bending tubular steel were kindred, essential operations, the center of his art. His work was always, in some primary way, about its own materiality, an address to the solidification of concrete rather than the concretization of fashion.

The Whitney—like the Guggenheim—is an investigation of a boldly sculptural form, part of an architecture conceived as mass—not, as with Graves, as surface. Breuer's take here extended well beyond the primary form of the object to the specific gravity of its constituents. The Whitney is an essay in architectural density, an extremely subtle and revelatory exploration of shades of gray, of texture, weight, and variation in stone and concrete. Breuer was scarcely alone in his fascination with this research. Le Corbusier's post-war production was formally centered on heroic sculpting in concrete. Likewise, Paul Rudolph was—at the time Breuer did the Whitney—pouring out his own fabulous concrete period. Indeed, a worldwide fascination with the stuff had come to bear the soubriquet Brutalism, a somewhat unfortunate play on the French for raw concrete, *beton brut*, a term reflecting the traditionally worshipful Gallic mystification of the natural (*eau sauvage*).

The Whitney is miles from brutality, light years from those rough-cast shrines to abrasion that gave Brutalism its bad name. This is a building about sequence, conceived modernistically—according to a "free plan." Virtually every moment is spatially imagined and dramatic. First comes the building's startling presence on the street. Breuer recognized both the scale and the jumble of that reach of Madison Avenue and made a building at once distinct and deferential. The flip side of its ingenious in-stepping excavation of the below-grade sculpture court and inflection (the current word) toward its entrance, is the out-stepping of the mass as it rises until its upper most part presses against the street-wall, like Marcel Marceau limning a window. In a time before cornice heights became a matter of legislation (the Whitney lies in the present Madison Avenue Special Zoning District) Breuer made a building whose top almost precisely accords with current wisdom as to where that line should be.

Recognizing the party-wall character of the row, Breuer divided his Madison Avenue elevation into three parts: a thin concrete wall butted up against its neighbors; a narrow zigzagging band containing, among other things, the great stair; and the main stepping mass, housing the galleries, to which are affixed the winning "eyebrow" windows, apt symbols of museum-going. This division into three has the additional effect (in concert with the lovely bridge and the splatter of windows) of pulling one's reading of the building off the symmetrical, reinforcing the strength of its corner.

Breuer's covered bridge makes one of New York's finest entries. Its angular form and cast concrete construction are reflected in the zigzag band containing the stair, a nice unity between the building's two primary icons of movement. Bridging the sculpture-filled moat, one glimpses behind it the social life of the cafe, a lovely introduction, and arrives in the slate-floored lobby space, both day-lit and illuminated by a beautiful array of silvered bulbs in saucer-shaped reflectors. From the lobby, one is offered three swell circulation experiences, a happy dilemma of potential progression. The options are: to go down a monumentalized open stair to the cafe and courtyard visible beyond; to go up in the gigantic elevator, that wonderful ascending room; or to enter the staircase.

As the stairway is one of the great architectural problems, Breuer's is one of the great solutions. On each floor the sequence begins with an orienting curved wall that sets up the experience in terms of direction, materials, and lighting. Then comes the stair itself, both complexly configured and perfectly, restfully modulated. Let me recall some fragments. The initial overlook to the street. The fine rail of metal and wood. The rhythm of compression and expansion of the space. The stone treads cantilevering out from the concrete armature, visible only from beneath. The investigation of adjacent values in materials, rough, smooth, dense, and less. The mysterious diffusion of light. The benches like altars. A helluva place.

PAGE 84

Finally the galleries. Their high rooms use strong textures of floor and filing as datums against which to register shifts in wall. The periodic surprise of the variously sized eccentric windows offers counterpoint to overall orthogonality. This is the building of a designer working at the height of his powers, a complete work of art, not alterable. Too young to be an official landmark, it's one in every other sense, an historic structure.

The Graves scheme leaves no aspect of the Whitney unvandalized. The overall strategy is to obliterate the building by rendering it subsidiary, turning it into no more than a subordinate part of a larger whole. At the level of massing, this is accomplished by adding a volume of similar size and height at the other end of the block, where it acts—along with the supressed original—like one of the bottom members of a human pyramid. On the backs of these two structures, Graves loads level after klutzy level of building, now a tier with little setbacks, now a tier with a cyclopean lunette, now a gross pergola, now a rustic cornice. It's a strategy meant to dazzle us out of so much as noticing the buried Breuer, a relentless assault of mass, materials, shapes, and phony style. Between the two bottom volumes is perhaps Graves's most inane and subversive invention, a stepped cylinder which has assumed one of those faux-naif monikers so beloved of architects: the hinge.

The hinge is pivotal. It centralizes the composition, erasing both the Breuer's own asymmetry and its asymmetrical relationship to the rest of the block. It further rationalizes the spurious balance between the original and its hulking doppelganger by picking up the Breuer's coursing and set-in lines and conveying them to its apish kith. To do this, it literally obliterates the two narrow vertical bands mentioned earlier and attaches itself to what remains, causing both sides of the composition to step down symmetrically from the middle of the block, a complete transformation of Breuer's intent. Affixed to the old Whitney like a goiter, the device obscures and intrudes on the stair and irrevocably blemishes the front facade.

In plan, the hinge provides the opportunity for a circular form which Graves uses to achieve several juvenile rotations off the grid and to create a lumber of cylindrical spaces. Breuer's original free plan has been overwhelmed by axial relations, banal symmetries, and facile scale tricks. The eyebrow windows no longer float in space, they're at the ends of corridors or trapped in little rooms like pigs in pokes. There are major axes and minor axes, chambers and antechambers, portals and vestibules, the whole shitty beaux-arts apparatus against which modernism rebelled. No doubt there will be the usual fey pastels and precious neo-conservative details as well. Absolutely nothing is left untouched. The curved stair-entries will go, as will the window. The big elevator will no longer serve. The cafe will be yanked up to the roof. Graves even proposes to dump steps into the sculpture court. The man's a kamikaze.

Whatever else he is, though, Michael Graves is surely a creature of the current climate, an architect for the age of Reagan. I imperfectly understand the institutional imperatives that make the Whitney want to tart itself up in the moth-eaten retro drag of Capitalist Realism, to make a museum that looks like a museum, but here's the proof that it does. The question now is how can it be stopped, how can a magnificent building be saved?

I think this scheme may be vulnerable. Not because it's unbearably, stupidly ugly (no crime here and besides, [Paul] Goldberger thinks it's a work of genius), but because it's bad of its kind and because it so clearly affronts everything that we hold dear, preservationwise. Looking at the drawings, it struck me that Graves's heart wasn't really in this: the plans and elevations were so dull, so filled with hackneyed figures and arrangements, the whole thing so autoplagiaristic, no better than a bad rip-off, looking like it was done in two weeks. Properly apprised of this, perhaps the Whitney will demur, call for a redo, not want to add a third-rate piece to its collection.

PAGE 85

More promising may be the preservation route. While the Breuer enjoys only weak protection, the adjoining brownstones cannot be destroyed without permission from the Landmarks Commission. Their demolition is defended by Graves on the grounds that the new building will "enhance the urban characteristics of the surrounding neighborhood." This, of course, is the old "we had to destroy it to save it" argument, of a class with the idea that we might as well tear down Paris since we've got a perfectly good facsimile down at Disney World.

PAGE 86

Graves himself identifies the key physical characteristics of the nabe as being small-scale and "figurative." This may or may not be true, but I can't see how this analysis jibes with banging in the equivalent of 20 stories and wiping out a fine group of traditionally figured remnants. I'm no knee-jerk preservationist, but if the only way to get this awful addition subtracted is to save those brownstones, let's save the hell out of them. Hands off the Whitney, Graves!

CHAPTER 3

WHAT'S WORTH PRESERVING

What makes a landmark? A landmark is defined as a building or other place of outstanding historical, aesthetic, or cultural importance, often declared as such by some civic authority. The first examples that spring to mind are obvious: libraries, museums, train stations, churches, state houses. The large-scale and beautiful institutions of urban and cultural life, most built over a hundred years ago. But what about the factories, built around the same time and equally imposing? What about the housing for the factory workers, the men and women who built the American economy? Or airports? The new building type of the second half of the twentieth century, so inspirational for architects but so quick to become obsolete. The idea of a landmark becomes fuzzier as we move closer to the present, but in most ways it becomes more interesting. What deserves to be preserved—and to what purpose—is more controversial when talking about a brutalist concrete parking garage of the 1960s than a neoclassical bank of the 1890s. Why should it be saved? What can be done with it? Is it even good architecture?

When writing about skyscrapers and museums, the critic is in effect suggesting future monuments, rendering judgment about where they rank on a historical scale. But when evaluating a potential landmark, the critic's role is more active: he or she is called upon to judge a much wider slice of the urban environment, and his or her words have the potential to change the shape and growth of the city. In critiquing a landmark, or a potential one, the critic has to engage with the street-level realities of city making: the history of the building and its neighborhood, the present-day context, questions about private ownership and the public good. Politicians, community boards, local activists, and developers all have to participate in a public process of architectural critique. The quality of the design, the reputation of the architect, the continuing usefulness of the type all play a part in the evaluation of whether or not an old, historic building becomes a protected landmark. Architecture critics who may stand on the aesthetic sidelines of urban affairs by circumstance or choice often become activists.

Activist criticism has a long history, and several of the critics whose work you have read in previous chapters have stepped into the role of activist at particular times. Ada Louise Huxtable was at the forefront of protests over the demolition of McKim, Mead & White's 1910 Pennsylvania Station in 1963, defining, for future critics, how one could be both a modernist interested in the future of architecture and a preservationist interested in the past. Lewis Mumford joined Jane Jacobs in her protest over plans to run a boulevard through Washington Square Park.

But some critics are outraged most of the time, and that anger structures their *approach* and suggests their *theme*. The principal difference between activist criticism and the pieces we have read so far is that the former makes an argument. While formal or experiential critiques describe, tour, demonstrate, and elaborate, the activist critique is structured like an editorial, stating its premise at the outset and proving—whether that a building should be torn down, that a building should be saved, or that an addition is a monstrosity—through historical background, visual data, and newsy reportage. Preservation and activist criticism go hand in hand, because a debate about whether to declare a building a landmark is one of the few times the critic can change the course of construction or destruction.

This chapter looks at two examples of activist criticism, one from the 1980s and one from the 2000s, and considers how to structure an effective argument for preservation. The first critic considered is Michael Sorkin, whose valiant defense of the Whitney Museum (a hard-to-love building that has been threatened by addition practically every decade) in New York City you have just read. Sorkin's piece "Save the Whitney" is from 1985, and while its landmark debates are still relevant, the postmodern addition with which the Whitney was then endangered is now history itself. To bring Sorkin's critique up to date, I offer *New York* magazine architecture (and classical music) critic Justin Davidson's 2009 critique "St. Anywhere," a defense of the eccentric architecture of yesterday and today and of its importance to the city fabric. Davidson, like Sorkin, uses his review of a single building to define his personal criteria for creating a landmark.

There are two historical essays on preservation that I have found useful in establishing a critical position in relation to preservation. The first is the 1903 essay "The Modern Cult of Monuments" by historian Alois Riegl, which defined a set of five "values" for conservation of art and architectural artifacts at the turn of the nineteenth century, when European cities began to evaluate the ruins in their midst. (The second is Huxtable's take on preservation, "Lively Original Versus Dead Copy," discussed on page 81.) The various meanings of Riegl's terms have long been fodder for art historians, but in this loose interpretation the values he identifies help the critic analyze the merits of and define a position relative to a potential landmark. Before writing or engaging as an activist, the critic must understand what makes a landmark for him- or herself.

Riegl's first category is *historical value*, indicating that something important happened there. Historical value is most often designated with the placement of a plaque—so-and-so was born here, this important treaty was signed here, on this spot such-and-such battle happened. Historical value is generally not a debate for architecture critics but rather for historians and curators.

The second category is more subjective: *artistic value*. Most of New York's initially designated landmarks had artistic value, like the Astor Library (1854) (now the Public Theater), in that they were designed by famous architects, with expensive materials and extensive ornament, for ceremonial and public purpose. It is the question of artistic value and differences in evaluating taste over time, that often become battlegrounds in determining which modern structures to preserve.

The third category is *age value*: things impressive in their decrepitude. The ruined tuberculosis hospital at the south end of Roosevelt Island comes to mind, especially when seen in contrast to the twenty-plus years of generic residential towers built at the island's north end. Industrial ruins are more prevalent in the United States than at the sites of the castles Riegl looked at, and a new crew of urban explorers spelunks (and then photographs) the remains of automobile factories, steel plants, and prisons. The most successful design exploitation of age value, in recent memory, is in parks, where industrial ruins become part of a new landscape.

The fourth category is *use value*: buildings that continue to work for their original purpose or that have managed to evolve with the times. Grand Central Terminal (1913) and the New York Public Library (1911) on Fifth Avenue are landmarks celebrated for their original and continuing role in urban life. Were the library to digitize every book, rendering a physical place to read them obsolete, its value might require re-evaluation.

The last of Riegl's categories is *newness value*, which we can relate to the search for new skyscraper superlatives—the highest, the greenest, the latest in technology. These brand-new qualities can give a building historical status long after they have been normalized.

Applying Riegl's set of values to some of the buildings mentioned in the introduction to this chapter leads to intriguing results: Penn Station originally had artistic value but lost it through years of unsympathetic renovation and the change in taste from Beaux Arts to modernism. Its use value as a contemporary train station was in question, since its tracks and concourses were underutilized in the 1960s and its owners wanted to sell its air rights to developers to build much taller towers. The Whitney Museum had newness value in its striking brutalist design, as well as artistic value for the same reason. But each time the museum's board considered architects for an addition, they questioned its use value: was it big enough, in square footage and gallery dimensions, to contain the future of American art? Recently, the answer was a decisive No, leading to the museum's decision to decamp for a new building on the High Line downtown.

Applying Riegl's values to a potential landmark offers a rough guide to which aspects of the architecture might become the approach for a review. Does it have newness value? Then stress the pioneering aspects of the material or construction technique. Artistic value? Describe it as alluringly as possible, putting its best foot forward. Use value? Argue for it on its pragmatic merits. Even if Grand Central Terminal weren't spectacular, it would be hard to create a better hub for subway and train, with public space and private commerce all provided under one roof.

To see Riegl's categories at work, we can turn to Huxtable's 1965 essay "Lively Original Versus Dead Copy." In it Huxtable lays out her criteria for preservation in the modern era, some closely related to Riegl's ideas:

> Preservation is the job of finding ways to keep those original buildings that provide the city's character and continuity and of incorporating them into the living mainstream. This is not easy. It is much simpler to move a few historical castoffs into quarantine, putting the curious little "enclave," or cultural red herring, off limits to the speculative developer while he gets destructive carte blanche in the rest of the city.

She articulates a position about the lives of buildings that is very different than the attitudes of previous generations. The loftiest and best use of a building is not as a museum piece (historical value) but as part of a city that continues to grow (use value). While designating a landmark is good, making it part of the living, breathing city is better. Huxtable sees no point in villages like Colonial Williamsburg or in saving a facade and destroying everything behind it. (The 2009 renovation of Henry Miller's Theater in New York City is an example of facadism, the latter approach. The historic front was preserved as a sort of perpetual stage set attached to a brand new "green" auditorium.) She would see no point in slavish reconstructions of decayed structures and no point in creating historic districts that cannot change. Buildings of different ages create a vibrant city (an argument Jane Jacobs would later expand and which is discussed in chapter 6), and all-new and all-old are equally destructive impulses. Huxtable's critique offers an argument about preservation in general, while Riegl's essay establishes a set of criteria for determining which buildings should be preserved.

When Sorkin began writing architecture criticism for the *Village Voice* in 1978, he was an anomaly in the field in that he did not write for a national publication. Influential architecture critics to date had written for major urban newspapers and magazines, and had gained authority from that institutional backing. The *Village Voice* was an insurgent newspaper (one that supported the community against authority and aimed to be an alternative to the *Times* for city news—a role filled today by proliferating blogs like *Gothamist*). Sorkin's colloquial style and antiauthoritarian slant—the fact that he had an explicit leftist position at all—reflect the politics of the paper for which he was writing. He consistently questioned the work, the politics, and the behind-the-scenes machinations of architectural powers like Philip Johnson, the Museum of Modern Art, the Landmarks Preservation Commission (LPC), and, famously, Paul Goldberger, then the *Times* daily critic. (Huxtable, whose work he admired, got a pass.)

Sorkin saw architecture as much as a game as an art form, a position bolstered by the fact that he began writing during a recession. Many of his *Voice* reviews, collected in the 1994 book *Exquisite Corpse*, discuss buildings unbuilt, exhibitions shown, controversies engaged, rather than specific three-dimensional works of architecture. Yet Sorkin was and is a practicing architect, and when he turned to the building form, he could be lyrical and highly specific about the experience and effects of being there. "Save the Whitney" showcases Sorkin's cynicism and poetics. Sorkin enters the landmark debate with a strong, historically based position on the qualities of modern architecture and the ironies of Marcel Breuer's career, slashing away at Michael Graves's work and the board that commissioned him, and methodically describing why the Whitney deserves a second look.

He begins with irony: "History seems poised to take its revenge on poor Marcel Breuer." His sarcastic tone is distinct from that of the other reviewers discussed in this book. That he will be making an argument is clear from his vocabulary: *Agincourt*, *victory*, *tit for tat*, *fate*, *Oedipal*, *murderous*. The preservation of the Whitney is a battle rather than an aesthetic stroll. As in Goldberger's review of Hearst Tower, the buildings and the architects are players on the stage. But Goldberger's take was aggrandizing, heroic, whereas Sorkin sees Breuer cut down to size and wants to reduce Graves in the same way. The affront to the building feels personal as well as political. Sorkin's colloquial language puts little distance between the critic and the reader and, like Muschamp's use of *you* in his Guggenheim Bilbao piece, is intended to make the situation seem imperative. Such violent language and an aggressive tone aren't necessary for activism (some might argue that you catch more flies with honey), but they do draw attention to the fact that action is required.

Rather than his tone, what may be more generally adaptable by other critics is the fact that Sorkin devotes these opening paragraphs to a reappraisal of Breuer's museum, some twenty years after its completion. Although praised at its opening by the country's most influential critics, the building did not become beloved like Frank Lloyd Wright's Guggenheim. Its dark color, its lowering brow, and its distinct aesthetic in a neighborhood of traditional architecture made it a confrontational presence on Madison Avenue. Sorkin puts the building in mid-1960s context, as part of a set of experiments in modernism and art display. (Even if you don't like it, there is a reason it exists as is, and this helps to establish its artistic value.) If people prefer the Guggenheim, Sorkin suggests, that's their right, but there is no value difference between the two. He goes on to propose that in hiring Graves, the Whitney's board is distancing itself from its own building, aesthetically and functionally, refusing to acknowledge its historic importance. In Sorkin's narrative Graves is merely a hired hand, one suggesting additions that obliterate the original's spirit.

Sorkin is trying to wrest the job of critic back from the museum board and explain the building to a new generation more steeped in the historicist architectural language of postmodernism than the brutalist language of modernism: "First comes the building's startling presence on the street. Breuer recognized both the scale and the jumble of that reach of Madison Avenue and made a building at once distinct and deferential." After establishing the Whitney's place in history, Sorkin shifts to describing its effectiveness in the present. The section of visual description shows Sorkin's skill as a formalist critic, but it is all in the service of his argument. If the Whitney is undervalued artistically, an effective analysis of how it works and why it works well might convince some onlookers to become fans. Sorkin does not take up the museum's rejection of the building as a place to show art (use value), because he considers that unworthy. Rather, he tries to make his reader see the building through his own eyes.

Sorkin's initial move is to explain why the Whitney is, in fact, a contextual building rather than an exercise of ego like Breuer's Grand Central Terminal tower (1968). He wants to prove that Breuer's Whitney was not itself a provocation: The Whitney may be a "startling" presence, but Sorkin describes Breuer's thought process from the inside out and points out all the ways the granite block fits in. Though it is taller than its neighbors, the base of the top section of the museum follows the cornice line of the adjacent brownstones—an inflection now de rigueur in any historic district. It also does not project in front of those buildings but rather carves out space behind the established street wall, achieving drama by shadow rather than sculptural form. The thin concrete wall Sorkin mentions in his analysis of the facade's vertical organization is further proof of sensitivity. To butt the new building against a brownstone—similar in tone, but not in texture—would indeed have been brutal. Instead, Breuer neatly delineates old from new, allowing each to coexist on either side of the wall.

Sorkin's final point is about emphasis: the Whitney is meant to be seen in the round. Like the Guggenheim, the Whitney makes the view as you come around the corner as important as the view from across the street, giving energy to a static block. Graves's addition would refocus attention on just the front, forcing the museum-goer into a relationship that privileges Madison Avenue.

Moving to the inside of the museum, Sorkin explains how Breuer wanted the visitor to see art and then uses the building as a setup for the way in which Graves destroys that experience. The staircase, which reads as an off-center vertical band on the facade, is darker and less grand than those of the Beaux-Arts museums, but it is meant to serve as a place of reflection and delivery—"benches like altars," "orienting curved wall"—when moving from floor to floor. It is an experience for the individual rather than as display, enhanced by the ability to look outside as you use the stairs. He has the least to say about the galleries because they are so simple: concrete floors, concrete grid ceilings, and between them white walls meant to showcase the large paintings of the 1960s American artists. Wide open spaces. The occasional window is a work of art itself.

The quality of the original firmly established, Sorkin turns to the addition proposal. Sorkin says at the outset that he doesn't like Graves's work and thinks his selection alone indicates a homicidal urge toward architecture on the part of the Whitney board. But he turns his critical eye toward the details of the architecture anyway, analyzing the interior and the exterior in terms of what they do to the neighborhood, the facade, the flow through the museum. This is clever, because it allows readers with different tastes to evaluate the future experience rather than just the clash of styles.

To design an addition to such a well-known, high-style building is a tricky thing. Too modest and you create a background building, the equivalent of urban wallpaper. Too assertive and you overwhelm the original. What is just right? Sorkin treats the Whitney and the Whitney 2.0 as two separate museums. He understands that once you add on to the Whitney (or to any other building), it becomes a different animal. This would be true of a new addition to an older building as well—think of Foster + Partners' 2010 addition to the Museum of Fine Arts, Boston. What was different about the Whitney situation was that neither its reputation nor that of Graves's work had yet solidified. Sorkin has to review 1960s modernist and 1980s postmodernism before they became history.

So, what's wrong? First, not only does Graves fail to defer, but he subjugates Breuer. Later attempts to add on to the Whitney by Rem Koolhaas (2001) and Renzo Piano (2004) would take very different approaches to the problem of adding to a landmark. Koolhaas proposed a looming, comma-shape structure that lofted a Breueresque block up into the air, doubling the good or bad impression one already had of the 1966 building. Piano proposed a background building along the lines of Gwathmey Siegel's rectangular white backdrop to the Guggenheim (1992), the bulk of which was set behind the adjacent brownstones. The latter was criticized as too respectful. Graves had no such problem. What makes Sorkin maddest is not just the size of the addition but the way it makes Breuer's corner-defining, asymmetric composition into a frontal, almost symmetrical one. He has described that irregular composition in clear, visual language, so now he expects the reader to understand what the addition destroys. In order to make his argument, he first spent much of the review on re-education.

The final element of the activist critique is politics, which Sorkin brings in at the end. Despite his efforts (and those of other critics), Sorkin doesn't think the Whitney has enough defenders based on its own merits. Those brownstones next door, which have historic value, could prove to be the nail in the scheme's coffin. The brownstones are ordinary buildings, but they are old and are part of the neighborhood fabric. The creation of the "historic district" designation was intended to preserve precisely this kind of character-building architecture. The quotidian has more protection—and more potential defenders—than Breuer's extraordinary structure, and Sorkin is willing to take what he can get. In his conclusion he transforms from a highly opinionated critic to an activist. The frank admission of where the real protection lies is part of his deflationary, colloquial strategy. He's not arguing from on high but from the trenches. He wants his readers not just to nod along with him but to do something about it.

Blair Kamin, long-time, Pulitzer Prize–winning architecture critic for the *Chicago Tribune*, writes in the introduction to his 2003 book *Why Architecture Matters*: "Activist criticism is based on the idea that architecture affects everyone and therefore should be understandable to everyone. Activist criticism invites readers to be more than consumers who passively accept the buildings that are handed to them. It bids them, instead, to become citizens who take a leading role in shaping their surroundings." Kamin, like Sorkin, challenges his readers to get involved in shaping their surroundings but understands that criticism needs to make the stakes clear. That's why activist criticism needs to provide historical context, offer a visual and easily understandable argument for the value(s) represented by the building in question, and outline what can be done. Preservation provides a perfect opportunity for critics to do something. It is a referendum on the past and a chance to assess the future of a building, an institution, and even a neighborhood.

(A final irony: Sorkin was right. The brownstones trumped Breuer. While Graves's addition, and the proposal by Koolhaas after it, foundered before they encountered the New York City Landmarks Preservation Commission [LPC], Piano was forced to preserve them. Piano's proposal was approved by the LPC in 2005 and the local community board in 2006—but not without modifications. He initially proposed demolishing two of the brownstones in order to create a broad entrance for the addition, set back from the street and the Breuer facade. To gain approval he had to rework the design to demolish just one row house. Piano and the Whitney board were never happy with this compromise, and in 2009 the museum chose not to fight but to move. They partly paid for their new downtown museum site by selling the brownstones.)

The Whitney falls into the category of odd duck. It is a building by a famous architect but without a critical or popular consensus on its worth. The Whitney has been saved, though its future contents are unknown, while Edward Durell Stone's Gallery of Modern Art (1964) at 2 Columbus Circle, another odd duck, was stripped and reborn as a very different kind of museum. A building that could be the third member of the mid-1960s oddball triumvirate, was also saved from the wrecking ball in 2010 by the bad economy. In 2011, new owners found that they could reuse it after all. The O'Toole Building, longtime home of St. Vincent's Hospital, was designed by architect Albert Ledner to be used as the headquarters of the National Maritime Union. Its scallop-edged projecting upper floors earned it the nickname "the overbite building," but it never had the elegance or pedigree of its contemporaries. (Have you heard of Ledner?) When, in 2009, it looked like the end was nigh, Davidson published "St. Anywhere" in which he argued for adding a new value to Riegl's list: eccentricity.

> When St. Vincent's hospital finally swings a wrecking ball at the O'Toole Building—the endearingly awkward, formerly white, three-layered stack with tear-off perforations and protruding upper floors on Seventh Avenue and West 12th Street—it will be for the greater good of Greenwich Village. The medical tower that rises in its place will serve the community and fortify the hospital's tottering finances.
>
> But this improvement comes at the cost of eccentricity.... As block after Manhattan block acquired a high-gloss sameness, the "overbite building," as it is known, has remained a folly, one of those defiantly impractical structures that somehow survived in this city's rugged real-estate ecology. Until now....
>
> Personality is endangered in New York architecture, though not totally extinct. Even as the mid-century misfits fade away—Edward Durrell Stone's 2 Columbus Circle; now the O'Toole—an occasional new one arrives. Cooper Union's still-unfinished academic center, designed by Morphosis, will never look demure. The white-glass schooner that Frank Gehry designed as headquarters for InterActiveCorp is hardly self-effacing, either. But imagine a few decades from now, if IAC should go the way of the National Maritime Union and the next owner chafes

at the strangely shaped and odd-size offices; then Gehry's flourish may turn into one more disposable trace of New York weirdness, scrapped to make way for something depressingly normal.

Davidson's review, like Sorkin's, is structured as an argument. While Sorkin's argument was for the Whitney in particular, Davidson uses the O'Toole Building as an example to make a larger case for eccentricity as an urban value. If Sorkin's theme was the Whitney's architectural excellence, Davidson's is redefining excellence. He doesn't use sarcasm, but instead a calm, reportorial tone that ultimately reads as melancholy.

I include Davidson's review for several reasons. First, to show that the battle for the preservation of modern architecture continues, and the question of landmark values is a recurring critical theme. Second, to show the potential for activist criticism to take on the theme of preservation at different scales. Both Sorkin and Davidson's reviews have a building at center, but the specific piece of architecture is put to different use. And last, to point out the similarity in structure. Both are activist critiques and structured as such: they begin with irony, follow with history and visual appreciation, and end with politics.

Davidson opens with the admission that the destruction of the building will be for the greater good of the neighborhood, which badly needs a new hospital (use value), but not for the city as an interesting place (artistic value). As at the Whitney, these two values are opposed, and it is up to the reader, and ultimately the LPC, to decide which one should win out. The O'Toole Building is at a disadvantage, however, as Davidson's brief history shows: it is no Whitney; and Ledner, no Breuer. As aforementioned, making landmarks of museums and other works by famous architects has always been easier than arguing for the preservation of lesser structures—*lesser* meaning less monumental, less pedigreed, less central. Davidson can't go on at length about O'Toole's artistic qualities but lets its nickname, "the overbite building," do the talking.

Davidson then segues into his larger theme: "Personality is endangered in New York architecture, though not totally extinct." Because his essay is as much about architecture in general as it is about O'Toole, he spends several paragraphs establishing the opposing visual characters of the "tastefully bland, well-tailored *facility*" that may correct the overbite, as well as new buildings that share its quirky personality. Eccentricity, like bad taste, is something most of us only know when we see it, and Davidson defines it through visual example, the same way Sorkin defined the difference between Breuer and Graves.

So what makes a landmark? Perhaps it has something to do with the buildings that are memorable. It can be the critic's role to help save them, by offering a broad and convincing argument for their worth, and insight into the politics of preservation. But the critic is only a single voice and may or may not become a rallying cry for wider urban or neighborhood activism. To be a good critic is to make the best possible argument for why the oddballs should be saved or built in the first place; to be a good citizen is to know them when you see them.

Davidson ends on a downbeat, unlike Sorkin, bowing to the "depressingly normal" imperatives of politics, economics, and healthcare. But by making this argument, setting a controversial theme, backing it up with visual data, and making architecture, as Kamin writes, "understandable to everyone," he has stepped out from behind the polite affect of formalist criticism and entered the urban fray. Whether to do so is largely a matter of personality, perhaps of historical circumstance, but it offers a possible role for critics on a larger stage than the newspaper.

CHECKLIST

1. Activist criticism works best when the critic feels strongly about the outcome. Identify a recent or ongoing preservation controversy in your area. Identify the stakeholders in the decision to preserve, modify, or replace. Who spoke in favor of the building and who against? What values, in Rieglian terms, were espoused by either side? Which value(s) would you have stressed and why? Are new values, like Davidson's eccentricity, required to properly assess the building's impact on the city?

2. Answer these questions in a piece of criticism by constructing an argument. Find your theme by asking questions like: Is this building important individually or as part of a larger urban example? Where does the greater public good lie, with preservation or demolition? State your point of view in your opening paragraph and then prove it through history, visual description, and political argument.

3. Other questions to consider: What is the history of building and how is that relevant to its current state? What are its good qualities? What are its drawbacks? Can you show (rather than tell) what makes it worth preserving? Who benefits from preservation or demolition? What are the real-world pressure points that could change the building's fate?

You Have to Pay for the Public Life

CHARLES W. MOORE

Perspecta 9/10 (1965): 57–106

This issue of *Perspecta* considers monumental architecture as part of the urban scene. I was asked to ferret out some on the West Coast, especially in California. *Perspecta's* editors suspected, I presume, that I would discover that in California there is no contemporary monumental architecture, or that there is no urban scene (except in a sector of San Francisco), or more probably, that both monumental architecture and the urban scene are missing. Their suspicions were well founded; any discussion from California in 1964 about monumental urban architecture (as it is coming to exist, for instance, in New Haven) is bound to be less about what we have than about what we have instead.

Any discussion of monumental architecture in its urban setting should proceed from a definition of (or, if you prefer, an airing of prejudice about) what constitutes "monumental," and what "urban" means to us. The two adjectives are closely related: both of them involve the individual's giving up something, space or money or prominence or concern, to the public realm.

Monumentality, I take it, has to do with monuments. And a monument is an object whose function is to mark a place, either at that place's boundary or at its heart. There are, of course, private monuments, over such places as the graves of the obscure, but to merit our attention here, and to be of any interest to most of the people who view it, a monument must mark a place of more than private importance or interest. The act of marking is then a public act, and the act of recognition an expectable public act among the members of the society which possesses the place. Monumentality, considered this way, is not a product of compositional techniques (such as symmetry about several axes), of flamboyance of form, or even of conspicuous consumption of space, time, or money. It is, rather, a function of the society's taking possession of or agreeing upon extraordinarily important places on the earth's surface, and of the society's celebrating their pre-eminence.

A version of this agreement and this celebration was developed by Jose Ortega y Gasset, in *The Revolt of the Masses*, into a definition of urbanity itself. "The *urbs* or *polis*," he says, "starts by being an empty space, the *forum*, the *agora*, and all the rest is just a means of fixing that empty space, of limiting its outlines."[…]

Ortega y Gasset's product is the city, the urban unit based upon the Mediterranean open square, a politically as well as physically comprehensible unit that people used to be willing to die for. The process of achieving an urban focus is the same as that of achieving monumentality: it starts with the selection, by some inhabitants, of a place which is to be of particular importance, and continues when they invest that place with attributes of importance, such as edges or some kind of marker. This process, the establishing of cities and the marking of important places, constitutes most of the physical part of establishing civilization. Charles Eames has made the point that the crux of this civilizing process is the giving up by individuals of something in order that the public realm may be enhanced. In the city, that is to say, urban and monumental places, indeed urbanity and monumentality themselves, can occur only when something is given over by people to the public.

PAGE 108

Planners have a way of starting every speech by articulating their (private) discovery that the public body's chief concern is people. The speech then says unrelatedly that it's too bad the sprawling metropolis is so formless. It might well be that if the shibboleth about people were turned inside out, if planning efforts went toward enlarging people's concerns—and sacrifices— for the public realm, that the urban scene would more closely approach the planners' vision, and that the pleasures of the people would be better served.

The most evident thing about Los Angeles, especially, and the other new cities of the West is that in the terms of any of the traditions we have inherited, hardly anybody gives anything to the public realm. Instead, it is not at all clear what the public realm consists of, or even, for the time being, who needs it. What is clear is that civic amenities of the sort architects think of as "monumental," which were highly regarded earlier in the century, are of much less concern today. A frivolous but pointed example is the small city of Atascadero, which lies in a particularly handsome coastal valley between Los Angeles and San Francisco. It was first developed in the '20s as a real-estate venture with heavy cultural overtones and extensive architectural amplification. Extraordinarily ambitious "monumental" architecture popped up all over the townsite. Buildings of a vague Italian Romanesque persuasion with a classic revival touch, symmetrical about several axes, faced onto wide malls punctuated or terminated by Canovesque sculpture groups. The effect was undeniably grand, if a bit surreal, exploiting wide grassy vistas among the dense California oaks. But there wasn't much of a town until the '40s. Then, on the major mall, an elaborately sunken panel of irrigated green, there cropped up a peninsula of fill surmounted by a gas station. Later, there came another, and more recently an elevated freeway has continued the destruction of the grand design. All this has happened during the very period in which Philadelphians, with staggering energy and expense, have been achieving in their Center City long malls north from Independence Hall and west from a point just off their City Hall, grand vistas at every scale, an architectural expression overwhelmingly serene, all urban desiderata which the Atascaderans did not especially want or need, and have been blithely liquidating. Doesn't this liquidation constitute some sort of crime against the public? Before we start proceedings, we should consider what the public realm is, or rather, what it might be in California now and during the decades ahead, so that the "monumentality" and the "urbanity" that we seek may be appropriate as functions of our own society and not of some other one.

In California cities, as in new cities all over the country (and in California just about all cities are new cities), the pattern of buildings on the land is as standard as it is explosive. Everywhere near population centers, new little houses surrounded by incipient lawns appear. They could be said to be at the edge of the city, except that there is no real edge, thanks to the speed of growth, the leapfrogging of rural areas, and the long commercial fingers that follow the highways out farther than the houses have yet reached. Meanwhile, in areas not much older, houses are pulled down as soon as zoning regulations allow, to be replaced with apartments whose only amenity is a location handily near a garage in the basement.

The new houses are separate and private, it has been pointed out: islands, alongside which are moored the automobiles that take the inhabitants off to other places. It might be more useful and more accurate to note that the houses and the automobiles are very much alike, and that each is very like the mobile homes which share both their characteristics. All are fairly new, and their future is short; all are quite standard, but have allowed their buyers the agonies of choice, demonstrating enough differences so that they can readily be identified during the period of ownership, and so that the sense of privacy is complete, in the car as well as in the house. This is privacy with at least psychic mobility. The houses are not tied down to any place much more than the trailer homes are, or the automobiles. They are adrift in the suburban sea, not so mobile as the cars, but just as unattached. They are less islands alongside which the cars are moored than little yachts, dwarfed by the great chrome-trimmed dinghys that seek their lee.

PAGE 109

This is, after all, a floating world in which a floating population can island-hop with impunity; one need almost never go ashore. There are the drive-in banks, the drive-in movies, the drive-in shoe repair. There is even, in Marin County, Frank Lloyd Wright's drive-in Civic Center, a structure of major biographical and perhaps historical importance, about whose forms a great deal of surprisingly respectful comment has already appeared in the press. Here, for a county filling up with adjacent and increasingly indistinguishable suburban communities, quite without a major center, was going to be the center for civic activities, the public realm, one would have supposed, for which a number of public-spirited leaders in the community had fought long and hard. It might have been, to continue our figure, a sort of dock to which our floating populace might come, monumental in that it marked a special place which was somewhere and which, for its importance, was civic if not urban. But instead of a dock for floating suburbanites, it is just another ship, much larger than most, to be sure, and presently beached (wedged, in fact) between two hills. It demands little of the people who float by, and gives them little back. It allows them to penetrate its interior from a point on its underside next to the delivery entrance, but further relations are discouraged, and lingering is most often the result of inability to find the exit....

During the years of California's growth, as its cities have appeared, the extravagances of the landscape and of the settlers upon it have suggested to many that straight opulence might create centers of the public realm. Three city halls, especially, clamor for our attention: The San Francisco City Hall probably heads the list for sheer expensive grandeur. The expensiveness was, one gathers, as much a political as a physical phenomenon, but the grandeur is a manifestation of the highly developed Beaux-Arts compositional skills of architects Bakewell and Brown. These great skills, though, have been curiously ineffectual in commending themselves to public concern. It is a curious experience, for instance, to stand in the towering space under the aggressively magnificent dome and to notice that hardly anyone looks up. And the development of the extensive and very formal civic center outside has had remarkably little effect on the growth of the downtown area, which has remained resolutely separate from all this architectural assertion. Surely a part of the failure to achieve an important public place here rests with the entirely abstract nature of the Beaux-Arts' earlier International Style. It takes a major master, like Sir Edwin Lutyens at New Delhi, to lift this idiom out of the abstract and to give some point to its being somewhere. The San Francisco City Hall demonstrates skill but no such mastery, so the city is not specifically enriched by this building's being here; it could be anywhere.

Or almost anywhere. It could not easily be in Gilroy. A small garlic farming community north of Salinas, Gilroy relied on a similar, if more relaxed, show of opulence in the building of its own City Hall in 1905. An elaborateness of vaguely Flemish antecedent served the town's desires; a truly remarkable array of whirls and volutes was concentrated here to signal the center of the public realm. But, alas, this concentration has not kept its hold on the public mind much more effectively than San Francisco's City Hall has, and now this fancy pile is leading a precarious life as temporary headquarters for the town's Chamber of Commerce and police station.

The citizens of Los Angeles adopted a slightly different route to achieve importance for their City Hall. In their wide horizontal sprawl of a city, they went up as far as seemed practical, and organized their statutes so no other buildings could go higher. But economic pressure has mounted, and now commercial structures bulk larger on the skyline than the City Hall. The Angelenos' vertical gesture should get some credit, in any case, for being a gesture, an attempt to make a center for a city which otherwise had none. As a formal gesture, it has even had some little hold on the public mind, although its popular image now involves a familiar tower rising in the smoggy background, while a freeway interchange fills the sharp foreground. Investing it with life, and relating the life behind its windows to the life of the city, may never have been possible; such investment, of course, has never happened.

PAGE 110

It is interesting, if not useful, to consider where one would go in Los Angeles to have an effective revolution of the Latin American sort: presumably, that place would be the heart of the city. If one took over some public square, some urban open space in Los Angeles, who would know? A march on City Hall would be equally inconclusive. The heart of the city would have to be sought elsewhere. The only hope would seem to be to take over the freeways, or to emplane for New York to organize sedition on Madison Avenue; word would quickly enough get back.

PAGE 111

Thus the opulence and the effort involved in the San Francisco, Gilroy, and Los Angeles City Halls all seem to come to very little in the public mind, lacking as they all do any activity which elicits public participation or is somewhat related to public participation. Whatever the nature of the welfare state, these public buildings seem to offer far less to the passer-by than such typical—and remarkable—California institutions as the Nut Tree, a roadside restaurant on the highway from Sacramento to San Francisco, which offers in the middle of a bucolic area such comforts as a miniature railroad, an airport, an extensive toy shop, highly sophisticated gifts and notions, a small bar serving imported beers and cheeses, a heartily elegant—and expensive—restaurant, exhibitions of paintings and crafts, and even an aviary—all of them surrounded and presented with graphic design of consummate sophistication and great flair. This is entirely a commercial venture, but judging from the crowds, it offers the traveler a gift of great importance. It is an offering of urbanity, of sophistication and chic, a kind of foretaste, for those bound west, of the urban joys of San Francisco....

PAGE 111

More recent years have their monuments as well. Indeed, by almost any conceivable method of evaluation that does not exclude the public, Disneyland must be regarded as the most important single piece of construction in the West in the past several decades. The assumption inevitably made by people who have not yet been there—that it is some sort of physical extension of Mickey Mouse—is wildly inaccurate. Instead, singlehanded, it is engaged in replacing many of those elements of the public realm which have vanished in the featureless private floating world of southern California, whose only edge is the ocean, and whose center is otherwise undiscoverable (unless by our revolution test it turns out to be on Manhattan Island). Curiously, for a public place, Disneyland is not free. You buy tickets at the gate. But then, Versailles cost someone a great deal of money, too. Now, as then, you have to pay for the public life.

Disneyland, it appears, is enormously important and successful just because it recreates all the chances to respond to a public environment, which Los Angeles particularly does not any longer have. It allows play-acting, both to be watched and to be participated in, in a public sphere. In as unlikely a place as could be conceived, just off the Santa Ana Freeway, a little over an hour from the Los Angeles City Hall, in an unchartable sea of suburbia, Disney has created a place, indeed a whole public world, full of sequential occurrences, of big and little drama, of hierarchies of importance and excitement, with opportunities to respond at the speed of rocketing bobsleds (or rocketing rockets, for all that) or of horse-drawn street cars. An American Main Street of about 1910 is the principal theme, against which play fairy-tale fantasies, frontier adventure situations, jungles, and the world of tomorrow. And all this diversity, with unerring sensitivity, is keyed to the kind of participation without embarrassment which apparently at this point in our history we crave. (This is not the point, nor am I the appropriate critic, to analyze our society's notions of entertainment, but certainly a civilization whose clearest recent image of feminine desirability involves scantily dressed and extravagantly formed young ladies—occasionally with fur ears—who disport themselves with wildest abandon in gaudily make-believe bordellos, while they perforce maintain the deportment of vestal virgins—certainly a civilization which seeks this sort of image is in need of pretty special entertainment.) No raw edges spoil the picture at Disneyland; everything is as immaculate as in the musical comedy villages that Hollywood has provided for our viewing pleasure for the last three generations. Nice-looking, handsomely costumed young people sweep away the gum wrappers almost before they fall to the spotless pavement. Everything works, the way it doesn't seem to any more in the world outside. As I write this, Berkeley, which was the proud recipient not long ago of a set of fountains in the middle of its main street, where interurbans once had run and cars since had parked, has announced that the fountains are soon being turned off for good, since the chief public use developed for them so far as been to put detergent in them, and the city cannot afford constantly to clean the pipes. Life is not like that in Disneyland; it is much more real: fountains play, waterfalls splash, tiny bulbs light the trees at night, and everything is clean....

Of course Disneyland, in spite of the skill and variety of its enchantments, does not offer the full range of public experience. The political experience, for instance, is not manifested here, and the place would not pass our revolution test. Yet there is a variety of forms and activities great enough to ensure an excellent chance that the individual visitor will find something to identify with. PAGE 111 A strong contrast is the poverty or absurdity of single images offered up by architects, presumably as part of an elaborate (and expensive) in-group professional joke. The brown-derby-shaped Brown Derbies of an earlier generation, which at least were recognizable by the general public, have given way to such phenomena as the new Coachella Valley Savings and Loan in Palm Springs which rises out of vacant lots to repeat Niemeyer's Palace of the Dawn, in Brasilia. Across the street from this, a similar institution pays similar in-group tribute to Ronchamp. The most conspicuous entry in this category of searches after monumentality, though, is architect Edward Durrell Stone's revisitation of Mussolini's Third Rome in Beverly Hills. This one has plants growing out of each aerial arch. Apparently there was a plethora of these arches, for they crop up again along Wilshire Boulevard, as far away as Westwood Village without, however, contributing much continuity to that thoroughfare....

For the opportunity, the actual commission to create a public realm, we must look to other sources than the Establishment of other times or other places, to people or institutions interested at once in public activity and in place. We depend, in part, on more Disneys, on men willing to submerge their own Mickey Mouse visions in a broader vision of greater public interest, and who are nonetheless willing and able to focus their attention on a particular problem and a particular place. Disneyland, however arbitrary its location, is unique, even as Los Angeles is, and much of its power over the imagination comes from the fact.

A chain of Disneylands would have a disquieting effect not unlike that of the new transcontinental chains of identical motels that weigh the tired traveler with the hopelessness of driving all day to arrive at a place just like the one he started from. One can hope, too, for the day when the gradual loss of differentiated place, the gradual merging of the gray no-places and the inundation of the places of special significance, will cause the slumbering citizenry to awaken, to demand to spend its money to have a public life. But it seems unwise to wait for that.

PAGE 115

Right now the largest single patron available to be pressed into the service of the public realm is the State Highway Department. Freeways until now have been one of the most serious generalizers of place in the state, ruthlessly and thoughtlessly severing some communities, congesting others, and obliterating still others, marring, gouging, and wiping out whole landscapes. Yet, for all that, they loom large in the public eye as one of the biggest, strongest, most exciting, and most characteristic elements of the new California. If one had to name the center of southern California, it would surely be the place not far from the Los Angeles City Hall where the area's major freeways wrap together in a graceful, strong, and much photographed three-level interchange (in the photographs, the tower of the City Hall rises through the distant smog). Much of the public excitement about San Francisco's small dramatic skyline is a function of the capacity to see it, a capacity which is greatly enhanced by the bridges (themselves major California monuments), by the freeways that lead to them, and now by the freeway that comes up from the south and breaks through the hills in the nick of time for a magnificent view of San Francisco. Indeed, in San Francisco as in few places, the view which gives a sense of the whole city is one of the most valuable parts of the public realm, one of the parts that is most frequently attacked and must be most zealously defended. One of the public views' most effective defenders could be the freeway builders, though admittedly, they have more often acted as saboteurs, as when they tried and partly succeeded, in San Francisco, in building a freeway wall between the city and the bay.

I am writing this in Guanajuato, a middle-sized town in the middle of Mexico, crammed into a narrow canyon, with just two narrow streets (one up and one down) in the bottom of the canyon, and with a maze of stepped pedestrian ways climbing up the canyon's slopes through the most remorselessly picturesque townscape this side of Greece. Under this runs a river, which used to inundate the city from time to time. Ten years ago a suburban portion of the river was still further depressed, and its former bed was lined with a handsome pink stone to serve as a canyon for cars, moving downhill above the river. Now, in a bold project happily called "the urbanization of the river," this development is being continued through the center of the town to let the river run with cars as well as water, sometimes behind buildings, sometimes under the ancient vaults over which the buildings of the town center spanned the river bed. None of the picturesque eighteenth-century delights is being threatened; a whole new twentieth-century layer of visual delights, at the scale of the automobile, is being added instead. The urbanity that results from this enlargement of the public realm is even more striking than the visual charm. The pedestrian spaces remain undefiled, even unattacked, while cars grind below, as in a miniature of a Hugh Ferris City of the Future that loses, miraculously, none of the delights of the past.

Guanajuato should offer us some lessons. The cities of California are much bigger, broader, and grayer, but then their budgets are larger, too (especially the items for freeway construction). They urgently need attention, before the characteristics that distinguish them at all are obliterated. There is no need and no time to wait for a not-yet-existent Establishment to build us the traditional kind of monuments or for a disaster gripping enough to wake the public conscience to the vanishing Places of the public realm we got for free. Most effectively, we might, as architects, first seek to develop a vocabulary of forms responsive to the marvelously complex and varied functions of our society, instead of continuing to impose the vague generalizations with which we presently add to the grayness of the suburban sea. Then, we might start sorting out for our special attention those things for which the public has to

PAGE 115

pay, from which might derive the public life. These things would not be the city halls and equestrian statues of another place and time, but had better be something far bigger and better, and of far more public use. They might, for instance, be freeways: freeways are not for individual people, like living rooms are and like confused planners would have you believe the whole city ought to be; they are for the public use, a part of the public realm; and if the fidgety structures beside them and the deserts for parking—or for nothing—under them don't yet make sense, it is surely because there has so far been too little provision for and contribution to and understanding of the public realm, not too much. The freeways could be the real monuments of the future, the places set aside for special celebration by people able to experience space and light and motion and relationships to other people and things at a speed that so far only this century has allowed. Here are structures big enough and strong enough, once they are regarded as a part of the city, to re-excite the public imagination about the city. This is no shame to be covered by suburban bushes or quarantined behind cyclone fences. It is the marker for a place set in motion, transforming itself to another place. The exciting prospects, not surprisingly, show up best at Disneyland. There, on the inside of the Matterhorn from the aerial tramway over the bobsled run on the inside of the plastic mountain, is a vision of a place marked out for the public life, of a kind of rocketing monumentality, more dynamic, bigger, and, who knows? even more useful to people and the public than any the world has seen yet.

PAGE 115

CHAPTER 4

SEARCHING FOR A CENTER

In 1965 architect Charles W. Moore was asked by the editors of *Perspecta: The Yale Architectural Journal*, to look for monuments in Southern California. He found none. Or none that conformed to the traditional architectural idea of a monument: an open square, a heroic statue, a flight of high steps, letters carved in stone. Such powerful, symmetrical, often neoclassical elements had historically come together to provide centers for civic life in Europe and the eastern United States. But in California, civic growth had come later, as a result of the success of the railroad and then the automobile. This meant that California's cities, particularly in the south, were wider and shorter than the cities of old, with low downtowns ringed by wide roads and single-family houses—what we call sprawl today.

When Moore began his *Perspecta* travel, he found the key cities on his trip had been emptied of people and that highways had become their most distinctive forms. He meant the title of essay about this search, "You Have to Pay for the Public Life" (1965), literally, in that he found urban experiences closest to those of New York or Boston in private developments like Disneyland, where you have to pay admission. He also meant it figuratively, in that public life does not come without individual economic sacrifice. Private homes, schools, shopping centers, and streets had become the building blocks with which cities were made. Moore was one of the first to ask what was lost by shrinking the public realm and one of the first to take commercial architecture seriously. (Another was Robert Venturi, whose essay

"Complexity and Contradiction in Architecture"—later a book—was published in the same issue of *Perspecta*. It would be seven years before he, Denise Scott Brown, and Steven Izenour published *Learning from Las Vegas*, their rigorous study of the architecture of the Strip.) The questions Moore raised have only become more pervasive in the decades since, as suburbs have grown, as monuments have modernized (from the Vietnam War Memorial to the World Trade Center Memorial), and as the lines between private and public space have blurred.

Moore's *approach* is a discursive travelogue that offers a sprawling alternative to the focused eastern newspaper review analyzed in earlier chapters. He moves from a discussion of the definition as well as the creation of monuments to the search for them and thus from an expositional journey to a physical one. This chapter splits into two parts: the first focused on Moore's style and quest; the second, on how his idea about the monument as being a creation by and for the people manifests itself in the work of other more recent critics like Michael Sorkin and Mike Davis.

Moore's style contrasts with the activist, even inflammatory, critique of downtown Los Angeles by Davis in *City of Quartz* (1990). Davis is a bit like Sorkin squared: deeply interested in the visual and physical structure of cities but always using what he sees to make a political point. Moore is determinedly apolitical, though his conclusions (and his architecture) undermine received wisdom about architecture of power. And yet Davis and Sorkin, both discussed below, echo Moore's thoughts about the need for gathering places and the emptiness of centers declared as such by fiat.

Just as important as an understanding of Moore's approach, though, is the contemporary application of his ideas. The central shock of his essay—an appreciation of the urbanism of Disneyland—is not really a shock in the post-postmodern era. What's more relevant is the quest for places, real and imagined, Moore might consider monuments today. The critical lessons in Moore are the effectiveness of this gentle, ironic, temporal approach, which is an approach that is a variant of Mumford's formal criticism at a California scale.

Davis looks at the Los Angeles spaces that are intended as monuments and also finds them wanting, but his approach is a direct and aggressive assault on critics and architects and planners who are willing to focus just on aesthetics:

Planners [in downtown Los Angeles] envision an opulent complex of squares, fountains, world-class public art, exotic shrubbery, and avant-garde street furniture along a Hope Street pedestrian corridor. In the propaganda of official boosters, nothing is taken as a better index of Downtown's "liveability" than the idyll of office workers and upscale tourists lounging or napping in the terraced gardens of California Plaza, the "Spanish Steps" or Grand Hope Park.

       In stark contrast, a few blocks away, the city is engaged in a merciless struggle to make public facilities and spaces as "unliveable" as possible for the homeless and the poor....

       ...One of the most common, but mind-numbing, of these deterrents is the Rapid Transit District's new barrel shaped bus bench that offers a minimal surface for uncomfortable sitting, while making sleeping utterly impossible....To ensure that ["Skid Row Park"] was not used for sleeping—that is to say, to guarantee that it was mainly utilized for drug dealing and prostitutions—the city installed an elaborate overhead sprinkler systems programmed to drench unsuspecting sleepers at random times during the night.

The street furniture and "exotic plantings" that in renderings transform a street in downtown L.A. into a free version of Disneyland's Main Street can be turned into weapons against less desirable populations. Davis, like Moore, offers different-colored glasses with which to look at public space.

    In this chapter, and the two that follow, the critics reverse their path, moving away from individual buildings and out into the surrounding spaces: monuments, parks, and neighborhoods. Moore puts the power to monumentalize in the hands of the people, not architects, building an argument for a new look at California's freeways, theme parks, and cul-de-sacs from the bottom up rather than the top down. Davis looks at what happens at the bottom, at what happens at the base of City Hall or when the wrong sort of people gather at the monument. And Sorkin proposes a public square, Liberty Square, as the best possible 9/11 memorial, arguing that a space to practice free speech and free movement is the best possible architecture versus terrorism.

When "You Have to Pay for the Public Life" was published, Moore was the dean of the Yale School of Architecture. In the 1960s, Moore and a team of collaborators designed Sea Ranch, the California coastal development, as a casual, weathered-gray village, using sloped roofs to blend the buildings into the scrubby, rugged cliffs. Inside some Sea Ranch buildings, bright supergraphics by Barbara Stauffacher Solomon served as art and walls, anchoring rooms that were open in plan (modern) and rough in materials (rustic). In New Haven Moore furthered these spatial experiments in his own residence, hollowing out a nineteenth-century house and replacing a traditional layout with layers of graphics and nested spaces that became central to the life of the architecture school. Home for Moore often involved a party, and his thoughts about where people like to gather were applied to both the public and private spheres.

Moore's urban work also combined strong, symbolic shapes and colors. His combination of American commercial design and European tradition was made most explicit at the Piazza d'Italia in New Orleans. That space, built in 1978 as a new city square around which development would materialize, had five concentric rings of columns with oversize Doric, Ionic, Corinthian capitals, a central fountain tiled with an iridescent map of Italy, water jets programmed as moving entertainment, and edges picked out in neon. The effect was cartoonish and brash, but its roots were in architectural tradition and Moore's sense of hospitality. The lessons Moore learned from Disneyland were reconfigured into a design that blurred the boundary between commercial and intellectual architecture. It was a space you could enter for free, but its delights were predicated on payments from developers.

Moore is anxious to be understood but too laid back to obscure his thought process. In "You Have to Pay for the Public Life," he writes as if he is thinking out loud, as if the reader were in the passenger seat of his car on the first day of his trip: "Monumentality, I take it, has to do with monuments. And a monument is an object whose function is to mark a place, either at that place's boundary or at its heart." His approach is quite different from that of the newspaper and magazine critics who start with the news, big statements about what has happened (in the case of Lever House's popularity) or what will happen (in the case of the Guggenheim Bilbao's popularity). Moore natters about the nature of his assignment, defining the terms for the reader as if he is just defining them for himself. This is likely a put-on, but it makes a slightly abstract quest immediately accessible. Rather than buttonholing his reader with an imperative "you," Moore chats you up, giving the sense we are all in it together, seeing the world around us with new eyes. Meanwhile, Moore moves swiftly in this introductory paragraph from describing the monument as a singular, inanimate object (the marker) to the monument as an active place and even social act. He defines the terms that his essay will explore, gently articulating a *theme* that may not become clear until the end. Architecture with a capital *A* had typically been used to make a monument, but Moore suggests that those designed spaces are empty of meaning if they are not accepted by society. His first hypothesis: people make monuments.

Common sense backs him up. We have all visited other cities and found ourselves in perfectly nice, totally deserted squares. Turn a corner and a much less physically attractive alley will be filled with lights and people and charm. The former was imposed by planners, architects, designers; the latter created by physical consensus. His line of thinking has much in common with that of Jane Jacobs. She too believes that spaces need to be adopted and adapted by people to be successful, and that bottom-up planning works better than top down. But she also tended to deny the possibility that architects and planners could learn from culturally created monuments. Moore was open to this same possibility, and this essay uses his learning curve to educate the reader.

As Moore continues his journey, he adds to his rough definition of *monumentality*. Publicly determined monuments are connected to the original foundation of cities: the selection of a single place from an undivided territory in which to create a community. Community and center are made together, in this narrative, by the coming together of people at a specific spot. Moore proposes a more social model, where the first architecture is a square (edges) or a statue (marker) for all to gather around. He paraphrases designer Charles Eames. To be in a civilization, a.k.a. be civilized, individuals have to realize they are better off together. They have to give up land or fuel or food to the greater good of society. But that was not what Moore saw happening in California in the 1960s or along the beltways of most major cities today: "The new houses are separate and private, it has been pointed out: islands, alongside which are moored the automobiles that take the inhabitants off to other places."

Here Moore turns to pointed visual description like that of the previous reviews, suggesting a new view of the suburban landscape as "a floating world." He generally avoids seeming like the authority, but these passages could not have been written by someone without knowledge of how California was made. (Note, however, that Moore doesn't explicitly critique this floating world or the style of those houses, banks, movie theaters.) He is interested in the behavior and the urban patterns that come from living in this world. Every home comes complete with everything the family needs, making neighbors superfluous and neighborhoods virtual. The distances, when experienced in the car, run together, so that fifteen minutes can take you to the cul-de-sac next door on local roads or across town on the highway. Whereas in the first sections of his essay Moore writes of history and tries to establish the ancient rationale for monuments, here he analyzes the present-day realities people lived in. He is not talking about a specific piece of architecture but the whole sea of buildings. He itemizes the elements of that reality—the houses dressed in every style, the cars parked out front, the drive-in amenities near and far— and arrives at a metaphor that allows him (and us) to make architecture of it.

Moore's essay was written in 1965 and focuses on California, two details that could make it seem remote from contemporary concerns. But his theme, you have to pay for the public life, is visible everywhere today. For Moore's writing to be an effective critical model, you have to understand how to apply his theme to your own experience.

In New York City, for example, the urbanized fruits of a collective mind-set are everywhere. Playgrounds rather than backyards, big public parks rather than small lawns, and subways rather than cars. In my neighborhood in Brooklyn there is a small lot, planted with grass and wildflowers that is called the Urban Meadow. For years it was a vacant, overgrown space, but once the city reclaimed it, neighbors stepped in to tame it, landscape architects improved it, and now it serves as a kind of group version of the suburban backyard. For $25 per year you get a key to a shed in the corner, access to a picnic table and plastic chairs, a grill, and a wading pool. You can have a cookout there or just hang out, but you have ten people using one grill ten times each, rather than 100 grills used 10 times a year. By Moore's definition the meadow is a monument, as a place of importance in the neighborhood (a small town within the big city), marked by flowers and trees, and symbolizing the giving up of individual yards and lawn furniture to the public good. The meadow also happens to be next door to a playground, an intended monument that is popular in its own way (although it lacks shade and grass and beauty), but only after school, and for parents of children under ten.

From the Urban Meadow, which shows that monuments can be modest, you can see the towers of Lower Manhattan jostling for position. One of the primary lessons of this essay is that one should look for monumentality in many more places. In New York, it was always commercial enterprise that built up, public life that built out. Skyscrapers create the look of the city from the air, but the parks and plazas in front of public buildings, like City Hall or the Metropolitan Museum of Art, form the landmarks of pedestrian life. As Moore describes it, Los Angeles went the opposite way: "The citizens of Los Angeles adopted a slightly different route to achieve importance for their City Hall. In their wide horizontal sprawl of a city, they went *up* as far as seemed practical, and organized their statutes so no other buildings could go higher." So late was the city to the skyscraper that the local politicians had the pick of the sky, erecting a tower and creating zoning to make it the tallest forever. He credits them with understanding what their city was lacking and trying to put architecture and planning at the service of creating a center. And it works in a pictorial sense: Los Angeles looks like *something* in the collective mind, in the fly-in establishing shots at the beginning of movies and from the freeway. The sidewalk critic might describe the pavement, the entrance, the Art Deco civic detail of City Hall, but Moore cannot be that critic. He experienced the city as Mumford did, as an everyman, but in California that makes him a critic from the car (also see Reyner Banham's *Los Angeles: The Architecture of Four Ecologies* [1971]).

Since it is the 1960s—the age of pickets and sit-ins—Moore muses on the other popular uses for civic squares: they can be public living rooms and public stages, places to celebrate and places to protest. In East Coast cities, civic squares would always have cameras focused on them—making a stand there resonates beyond the immediate onlookers. In Los Angeles, the cameras are on the back lots and in the studios, maybe at the beach. Nobody is looking at City Hall. A traffic jam: that would get coverage, but again, from the air. The lack of a place to protest is not a small problem, it is a symptom of the big problem he has been discussing from the start. Life in California is so fragmented, it is only on an artificial and private island that people converge: "Curiously, for a public place, Disneyland is not free. You buy tickets at the gate. But then, Versailles cost someone a great deal of money, too. Now, as then, you have to pay for the public life." At Disneyland the price you pay is explicit (it is written right up there on the sign), whereas for traditional public life the price is paid in taxes, in lack of privacy, and sometimes in forfeiting lawn for sidewalk. Since southern California governments haven't made these qualities a priority, the public realm hasn't developed into a free public life. The only way to re-create the sense of remembered pedestrian unity is to take on a role, pretending to be part of a community for just one day, trying it on for size.

The key word in Moore's Disneyland description is *play-acting*. Disney property is not public, though it has the form of Main Street and the open square we recognize from the nineteenth-century American towns. "Disneyland, in spite of the skill and variety of its enchantments, does not offer the full range of public experience," Moore writes. "The political experience, for instance, is not manifested here, and the place would not pass our revolution test." Were you to try to start a revolution, Minnie and Goofy would hustle you off to the exit. Moore, who has described the monument in historical context and in the present day, here veers into the future: a diagnosis has been rendered, but now the sick city needs a cure. As he motors along, reader in tow, he comes to a point where thinking out loud—cruising will no longer do. Even the travelogue needs to come to a conclusion.

The gray line between public and private space, and the increasing disappearance of the former in 1980s California, is the subject of "Fortress L.A.," the fourth chapter in Davis's *City of Quartz*. This chapter updates the "floating islands" Moore described: in the 1980s they become fortified. Davis writes,

> The carefully manicured lawns of Los Angeles's Westside sprout forests of ominous little signs warning: "Armed Response!" Even richer neighborhoods in the canyons and hillsides isolate themselves behind walls guarded by gun-toting private police and state-of-the-art electronic surveillance. Downtown, a publicly-subsidized "urban

renaissance" has raised the nation's largest corporate citadel [the
Bonaventure Hotel and Shopping Mall], segregated from the poor
neighborhoods around it by a monumental architectural glacis.
In Hollywood, celebrity architect Frank Gehry, renowned for his
"humanism," apotheosizes the siege look in a library designed to
resemble a foreign legion fort.

In Davis's Los Angeles, it is not merely space that keeps people apart but
the threat of violence. He finds that contemporary urban theory has been silent on
the "militarization of city life," while the movies have projected the violence into
postapocalyptic futures. Davis sets about his alternate tour of Los Angeles sites with
more of an agenda than Moore—his prose bristles while Moore's glides—but the
idea is similar: to see what is happening to the public on the ground.

Davis's first stop is downtown, at the base of City Hall and the towers
Moore observed from the freeway. Planners have imagined a friendly, green, and
"soft" environment of fountains, sculpture, and benches to tempt office workers
and tourists to congregate outdoors. But a few blocks away, another series of design
choices (like the "bumproof" benches and sprinklers described earlier) have isolated
the homeless people who are the area's primary residents. Restaurant garbage is
padlocked and public bathrooms eliminated. The result is a bifurcated "public" space,
welcoming some, alienating others, with most amenities moved into private hands.

This lack of clarity about what is public and what is private is one of
Davis's most perceptive points: it is the fuzziness about who owns the space
that makes it possible to deny access, either physically or psychologically, to
"undesirables." Davis cites William H. Whyte's pioneering 1980 study, *The Social
Life of Small Urban Space*s to describe that humans are social beings: they want to sit
in parks with other people, and they don't want to go where they are not wanted.
Whyte writes, "fear proves itself."

The politicians, planners, and police in Los Angeles use socialization as a
weapon. Why? Davis ultimately decides all of the fortification is the result of a fear of
crowds: "As we have seen, the designers of malls and pseudo-public space attack the
crowd by homogenizing it. They set up architectural and semiotic barriers to filter

out 'undesirables.' They enclose the mass that remains, directing its circulation with behaviorist ferocity."

Moore's subdued irony regarding the fact that revolution could not be fomented at Disneyland becomes, in Davis's prose, a street fighter's lament. Davis consistently uses the language of violence (*ferocity*, *attack*) to describe the (typically unidentified) planners' project. At no point is that more obvious than in the "Frank Gehry as Dirty Harry" section of the chapter, in which he takes Gehry to task for his "baroquely fortified" Goldwyn Library (1984) in Hollywood. Davis writes, "Gehry accepted a commission to design a structure that was inherently 'vandalproof.' The curiosity, of course, is his rejection of the low-profile, high-tech security systems that most architects subtly integrate in their blueprints. He chose instead a high-profile, low-tech approach that maximally foregrounds the security functions as motifs of the design." The fortifications include "its fifteen-foot security walls of stucco-covered concrete block, its anti-graffiti barricades covered in ceramic tile, its sunken entrance protected by ten-foot steel stacks." The Goldwyn Library, Davis decides, "projects the same kind of macho exaggeration as Dirty Harry's 44 Magnum."

It is strong stuff and more easily dismissed for its over-the-top accusations. But like Moore, Davis gets his reader to see the city in a new way, to look beyond the lawn at the sprinklers, to regard the bench as aggressive rather than a design object. It is a different energy applied to criticism and one that puts people (as well as pop-culture reference) first.

The strategies Davis observed in Los Angeles in the 1980s became more relevant to all cities in the wake of 9/11, when security became a rationale for a long list of defensive retrofits: the elimination of benches and trash cans, the addition of bollards around buildings and plazas, the presence of armed guards, and the appearance of I.D. checkpoints. Each step either architecturally or semiotically warned all but necessary personnel out of buildings and formerly public spaces. It became harder to get around and the effort less rewarding. New York, in becoming fortified, was losing some of its difference, and its monuments some of their political power as monument.

In a 2004 *Architectural Record* essay, "Finding an Open Space for the Exercise of Democracy in New York's Dense Urban Fabric," Sorkin raised a point that relates to both Moore's and Davis's accounts of privately owned public space, identifying the fact that despite the abundance of public streets and parks in New York City, there are few places for a large political rally. At the time the group United for Peace and Justice had just been denied permission to rally in Central Park during the Republican National Convention. The West Side Highway was offered as an alternative location, but the organizers rejected the suggestion as being too far from the center. Sorkin argued that more and more public spaces were being deradicalized, cut off from the possibility of becoming gathering places (or revolutionary sites) by the architecture of the War on Terror. Bollards, lack of amenities, guards, all turn what was public into private, and even the design of Ground Zero, created during a time of fear, chopped the sixteen acres into a number of pieces labeled Liberty, Freedom, and Light that offered little real freedom of movement.

Sorkin offered an alternative, one that seems straight out of Moore's essay from forty years earlier and a direct response to the fear of crowds Davis describes. If people have the power to create a monument, as these three writers indicate they do, they also have the power to create a movement: space and politics are inextricably linked. Sorkin writes:

> These blocks might become the great public plaza that the city lacks. Surrounded by a strong edge of buildings, highly accessible, and located on a site of remarkable resonance, the space might become not simply a symbol but the scene of liberty in action, a zone of free assembly and free speech....Instead of managing remembrance through a series of themed activities that offer little opportunity for spontaneity or collectivity, it would truly belong to the people, an embodiment of our nation's greatest ethical and political power.
> It's time to build Liberty Square.

Liberty Square has not happened, and the plans for Ground Zero proceed slowly toward their chopped-up, symbolic completion. Whether or not the memorial proves to be a real monument remains to be seen. But in the meantime, Moore's concluding thoughts about the structure of place, and the public life we have paid for, have come to architectural fruition: "If one had to name the center of southern California, it would surely be the place not far from the Los Angeles City Hall where the area's major freeways wrap together in a graceful, strong and much-photographed three-level interchange."

The freeway: not a destroyer of public space but an unconsidered openness, a monument by function of its public funding and its agreed-upon importance. At the time Moore was writing, consideration of the realm of the automobile (like the realm of Disney) as architecture was fairly heretical. A few architects, like Paul Rudolph, had designed heroic parking garages along the model of Le Corbusier's Couvent de la Tourette, but the roads themselves belonged to the American political dream of mobility and millions. During his travels over them, Moore began to see them differently, even cinematically: "Here are structures big enough and strong enough, once they are regarded as part of the city, to re-excite the public imagination about the city."

The future of the monument is in harnessing the qualities that *do* seem to matter to people in their everyday lives and in seeking inspiration in the built environment that had previously been seen as the periphery. From the Los Angeles freeway you can see City Hall, but you can also see the freeway itself. The building points backward; the road, forward. It is hard to tell if Moore is being serious or tongue-in-cheek. Does he really believe the freeways are future monuments or just that we need to start taking our public investments seriously?

I would suggest that contemporary architects have taken him at his word. There are a number of recent and upcoming architecture projects in which the space and light and motion of the highway are incorporated into potential new monuments and reincorporated into the walkable city. These examples apply Moore's theme, as distinct from his approach, as a way of extending his consideration of monumentality.

To write like Moore you have to see the world, at least for a time, through his eyes, and this chapter concludes with an applied description of what Moore might see as a potential freeway-as-monument. Moore's points can be oblique (his conversational tone has tripped up my students), but I want to point out how, in one case, architects adapted his final idea, freeway-as-monument, as design concept.

The first is a building. Thom Mayne, principal of the Los Angeles firm Morphosis Architects, has developed a body of built work that draws its strength from the size and movement of the California highway system. His buildings operate at a skyscraper scale despite being shaped more like wedges than towers. They use the materials of the street, metal panels and concrete, fragile glass protected by perforated screens from both sun and breakage. They look as if they were still moving by virtue of slashed facades, canted walls, and ground-level piloti, suggesting liftoff. All these tricks are in effect at 41 Cooper Square, Morphosis's 2009 academic building for Cooper Union, where diagonal concrete columns suggest on-ramps (especially to skateboarders), and the slowly undulating facade suggests vertical topography.

The second is a park. The FDR Drive, which follows the east side of Manhattan, has long been a barrier to access to the East River. Thin pedestrian bridges cross it periodically, but for most of its length, the pedestrian meets it either as a barricaded sea of traffic or as a dark elevated highway, sheltering pigeons and parking. Such limited and dispersed access has long made the thin parks between the FDR and the East River underused and potentially dangerous. When the city commissioned new plans for the East River Waterfront Esplanade (ERW) in 2004, the architects involved (the Richard Rogers Partnership, SHoP Architects, and Ken Smith Landscape Architect) considered burying the FDR, as it already descends into a trench around the lower tip of Manhattan, a few blocks south of the project site. The FDR is a classic case of the freeway as barrier, preventing a string of neighborhoods from accessing, and sometimes even seeing, the waterfront nearby. But the designers ultimately rejected this idea as too costly and suggested the city turn an impediment into an asset, the barrier into a path. In this case architects and government planners were acting like members of Moore's communities, trying to make underused infrastructure into a place people want to be. It also demonstrated a designer's response to Moore's question of what makes a monument.

In a traditional park, trees form a canopy over paths, encircle open spaces, and form a border between park and city. On the ERW (three blocks of which, designed by SHoP and Smith, opened in Summer 2011) the FDR has been drawn in to perform the same function. The dank and unconsidered lower surface of the highway has been cleaned and a pale purple girder added that is illuminated at night like a band of light. In one section it serves as a roof for a modernist dog run. New paving, in a pattern based on light bouncing off of the water, runs between the highway and the water's edge. There are planted swales, steps down to the water, and high benches, as at a bar, that allow you to belly up to the view of Brooklyn. In the future, landscaped streets on the west side of the highway will act as on-ramps to the park, imitating the materials and plantings of the ERW. On one pier SHoP created topography with a bilevel structure, with a planted upper story and a cafe below. The strength of the design, when it is finally complete, will come from precisely the conceptual leap Moore suggests: the designers took a big structure seen as outside the livable city and acclimated it to urban life. The ERW can never be physically central, but it could become the psychological center of an increasingly residential neighborhood.

Public life, public space, and how to make places that bring people together are the common themes in the writings of Moore, Davis, and Sorkin. All three believe in the power of people to designate or destroy monuments, bring safety to the streets, and create action through assembly. Moore's approach, as described here, is to embed critique into what appears to be a driving tour, thinking out loud as he moves from site to site but ultimately coming to a powerful conclusion about the monumentality of infrastructure. Davis seeks monuments only to destroy them, or to show how urban conditions have made assembly, sociability, even sitting, impossible in ostensibly public spaces. Sorkin suggests that space for assembly is the only possible monument for post-9/11 New York. As a gesture toward the applicability of these critics' themes to the contemporary scene, I offer descriptions of where monumentality is to be found in my city, both in the neighborhood and on the waterfront. The message of Moore is keeping your eyes open for public life, wherever you travel.

CHECKLIST

1. Identify three related public places or spaces in your city. Travel to them—on foot, by car, via public transportation—and describe the journey as well as the destinations. How is each space embedded in its urban fabric? Is it welcoming? Is it fortified? Who owns the space, and how is that ownership visible (or not)? Who occupies the space? Is it a monument?

   In writing this journey, try to stay in the moment of observation and description. Describe what you see. Describe what is happening in these spaces now and how it contributes (or not) to public life.

2. Find a fortified public space and analyze the way design has become a barrier. What benign elements have been adapted? Is the line between public and private blurred? In its current condition, who does the space attract and who does it repel?

3. Make your own search for monuments. Think about unlikely gathering places— the parking lot that becomes an international bazaar on the weekend, the former factory transformed into a graffitied art colony—any example of large-scale and unattractive public works that have become social spaces. Ask yourself: How did they get that way? Why this underpass rather than another one? What qualities of location, architecture, and/or programming allowed them to turn from path to monument? Are these qualities replicable in other locations?

4. Can freeways become monuments? Have they already become so? Argue for or against.

Public Parks and the Enlargement of Towns

FREDERICK LAW OLMSTED

A paper read at the Lowell Institute, Boston, FEBRUARY 25, 1870

...Of the fact of the general townward movement of the civilized world, and its comprehensiveness, there can be no doubt....

We have reason to believe, then, that towns which of late have been increasing rapidly on account of their commercial advantages, are likely to be still more attractive to population in the future; that there will in consequence soon be larger towns than any the world has yet known, and that the further progress of civilization is to depend mainly upon the influences by which men's minds and characters will be affected while living in large towns.

Now, knowing that the average length of the life of mankind in towns has been much less than in the country, and that the average amount of disease and misery and of vice and crime has been much greater in towns, this would be a very dark prospect for civilization, if it were not that modern Science has beyond all question determined many of the causes of the special evils by which men are afflicted in towns, and placed means in our hands for guarding against them. It has shown, for example, that under ordinary circumstances, in the interior parts of large and closely built towns, a given quantity of air contains considerably less of the elements which we require to receive through the lungs than the air of the country or even of the outer and more open parts of a town, and that instead of them it carries in to the lungs highly corrupt and irritating matters, the action of which tends strongly to vitiate all our sources of vigor....

It is evident that if we go on in this way, the progress of civilized mankind in health, virtue, and happiness will be seriously endangered....

Is this a small matter—a mere matter of taste; a sentimental speculation?

It must be within the observation of most of us that where, in the city, wheel-ways originally twenty feet wide were with great difficulty and cost enlarged to thirty, the present width is already less nearly adequate to the present business than the former was to the former business; obstructions are more frequent, movements are slower and oftener arrested, and the liability to collision is greater. The same is true of sidewalks. Trees thus have been cut down, porches, bow-windows, and other encroachments removed but every year the walk is less sufficient for the comfortable passing of those who wish to use it.

It is certain that as the distance from the interior to the circumference of towns shall increase with the enlargement of their population, the less sufficient relatively to the service to be performed will be any given space between buildings.

In like manner every evil to which men are specially liable when living in towns, is likely to be aggravated in the future, unless means are devised and adapted in advance to prevent it.

Let us proceed, then, to the question of means, and with a seriousness in some degree befitting a question, upon our dealing with which we know the misery or happiness of many millions of our fellow-beings will depend.

We will for the present set before our minds the two sources of wear and corruption which we have seen to be remediable and therefore preventible. We may admit that commerce requires that in some parts of a town there shall be an arrangement of buildings, and a character of streets and of traffic in them which will establish conditions of corruption and of irritation, physical and mental. But commerce does not require the same conditions to be maintained in all parts of a town.

Air is disinfected by sunlight and foliage. Foliage also acts mechanically to purify the air by screening it. Opportunity and inducement to escape at frequent intervals from the confined and vitiated air of the commercial quarter, and to supply the lungs with air screened and purified by trees, and recently acted upon by sunlight, together with the opportunity and inducement to escape from conditions requiring vigilance, wariness, and activity toward other men—if these could be supplied economically, our problem would be solved.

In the old days of walled towns all tradesmen lived under the roof of their shops, and their children and apprentices and servants sat together with them in the evening about the kitchen fire. But now that the dwelling is built by itself and there is greater room, the inmates have a parlor to spend their evenings in; they spread carpets on the floor to gain in quiet, and hang drapery in their windows and papers on their walls to gain in seclusion and beauty. Now that our towns are built without walls, and we can have all the room that we like, is there any good reason why we should not make some similar difference between parts which are likely to be dwelt in, and those which will be required exclusively for commerce?

Would trees, for seclusion and shade and beauty, be out of place, for instance, by the side of certain of our streets? It will, perhaps, appear to you that it is hardly necessary to ask such a question, as throughout the United States trees are commonly planted at the sides of streets. Unfortunately, they are seldom so planted as to have fairly settled the question of the desirableness of systematically maintaining trees under these circumstances. In the first place, the streets are planned, wherever they are, essentially alike. Trees are planted in the space assigned for sidewalks, where at first, while they are saplings, and the vicinity is rural or suburban, they are not much in the way, but where, as they grow larger, and the vicinity becomes urban, they take up more and more space, while space is more and more required for passage. That is not all. Thousands and tens of thousands are planted every year in a manner and under conditions as nearly certain as possible either to kill them outright, or to so lessen their vitality as to prevent their natural and beautiful development, and to cause premature decrepitude. Often, too, as their lower limbs are found inconvenient, no space having been provided for trees in laying out the street, they are deformed by butcherly amputations. If by rare good fortune they are suffered to become beautiful, they still stand subject to be condemned to death at any time, as obstructions in the highway.

What I would ask is, whether we might not with economy make special provision in some of our streets—in a twentieth or a fiftieth part, if you please, of all—for trees to remain as a permanent furniture of the city? I mean, to make a place for them in which they would have room to grow naturally and gracefully. Even if the distance between the houses should have to be made half as much again as it is required to be in our commercial streets, could not the space be afforded? Out of town space is not costly when measures to secure it are taken early. The assessments for benefit where such streets were provided for, would, in nearly all cases, defray the cost of the land required. The strips of ground reserved for the trees, six, twelve, twenty feet wide, would cost nothing for paving or flagging.

The change both of scene and of air which would be obtained by people engaged for the most part in the necessarily confined interior commercial parts of the town, on passing into a street of this character after the trees had become stately and graceful, would be worth a good deal. If such streets were made still broader in some parts, with spacious malls, the advantage would be increased. If each of them were given the proper capacity, and laid out with laterals and connections in suitable directions to serve as a convenient trunk-line of communication between two large districts of the town or the business centre and the suburbs, a very great number of people might thus be placed every day under influences counteracting those with which we desire to contend.

These, however, would be merely very simple improvements upon arrangements which are in common use in every considerable town. Their advantages would be incidental to the general uses of streets as they are. But people are willing very often to seek recreation as well as receive it by the way. Provisions may indeed be made expressly for recreation, with certainty that if convenient, they will be resorted to.

We come then to the question: what accommodations for recreation can we provide which shall be so agreeable and so accessible as to be efficiently attractive to the great body of citizens, and which, while giving decided gratification, shall also cause those who resort to them for pleasure to subject themselves, for the time building, to conditions strongly counteractive to the special enervating conditions of the town?....

If I ask myself where I have experienced the most complete gratification of this instinct in public and out of doors, among trees, I find that it has been in the promenade of the Champs Elysées. As closely following it I should name other promenades of Europe, and our own upon the New York parks. I have studiously watched the latter for several years. I have several times seen fifty thousand people participating in them; and the more I have seen of them, the more highly have I been led to estimate their value as means of counteracting the evils of town life.

Consider that the New York Park and the Brooklyn Park are the only places in those associated cities where, in this eighteen hundred and seventieth year after Christ, you will find a body of Christians coming together, and with an evident glee in the prospect of coming together, all classes largely represented, with a common purpose, not at all intellectual, competitive with none, disposing to jealousy and spiritual or intellectual pride toward none, each individual adding by his mere presence to the pleasure of all others, all helping to the greater happiness of each. You may thus often see vast numbers of persons brought closely together, poor and rich, young and old, Jew and Gentile. I have seen a hundred thousand thus congregated, and I assure you that though there have been not a few that seemed a little dazed, as if they did not quite understand it, and were, perhaps, a little ashamed of it, I have looked studiously but vainly among them for a single face completely unsympathetic with the prevailing expression of good nature and light-heartedness.

Is it doubtful that it does men good to come together in this way in pure air and under the light of heaven, or that it must have an influence directly counteractive to that of the ordinary hard, hustling working hours of town life?

You will agree with me, I am sure, that it is not, and that opportunity, convenient, attractive opportunity, for such congregation, is a very good thing to provide for, in planning the extension of a town....

PAGE 137

If the great city to arise here is to be laid out little by little, and chiefly to suit the views of land-owners, acting only individually, and thinking only of how what they do is to affect the value in the next week or the next year of the few lots that each may hold at the time, the opportunities of so obeying this inclination as at the same time to give the lungs a bath of pure sunny air, to give the mind a suggestion of rest from the devouring eagerness and intellectual strife of town life, will always be few to any, to many will amount to nothing.

But is it possible to make public provision for recreation of this class, essentially domestic and secluded as it is?

It is a question which can, of course, be conclusively answered only from experience. And from experience in some slight degree I shall answer it. There is one large American town, in which it may happen that a man of any class shall say to his wife, when he is going out in the morning: "My dear, when the children come home from school, put some bread and butter and salad in a basket, and go to the spring under the chestnut-tree where we found the Johnsons last week. I will join you there as soon as I can get away from the office. We will walk to the dairy-man's cottage and get some tea, and some fresh milk for the children, and take our supper by the brook-side"; and this shall be no joke, but the most refreshing earnest.

There will be room enough in the Brooklyn Park, when it is finished, for several thousand little family and neighborly parties to bivouac at frequent intervals through the summer, without discommoding one another, or interfering with any other purpose, to say nothing of those who can be drawn out to make a day of it, as many thousand were last year. And although the arrangements for the purpose were yet very incomplete, and but little ground was at all prepared for such use, besides these small parties, consisting of one or two families, there came also, in companies of from thirty to a hundred and fifty, somewhere near twenty thousand children with their parents, Sunday-school teachers, or other guides and friends, who spent the best part of a day under the trees and on the turf, in recreations of which the predominating element was of this neighborly receptive class. Often they would bring a fiddle, flute, and harp, or other music. Tables, seats, shade, turf, swings, cool spring-water, and a pleasing rural prospect, stretching off half a mile or more each way, unbroken by a carriage road or the slightest evidence of the vicinity of the town, were supplied them without charge, and bread and milk and ice-cream at moderate fixed charges. In all my life I have never seen such joyous collections of people. I have, in fact, more than once observed tears of gratitude in the eyes of poor women, as they watched their children thus enjoying themselves.

The whole cost of such neighborly festivals, even when they include excursions by rail from the distant parts of the town, does not exceed for each person, on an average, a quarter of a dollar; and when the arrangements are complete, I see no reason why thousands should not come every day where hundreds come now to use them; and if so, who can measure the value, generation after generation, of such provisions for recreation to the over-wrought, much-confined people of the great town that is to be?

For this purpose neither of the forms of ground we have heretofore considered are at all suitable. We want a ground to which people may easily go after their day's work is done, and where they may stroll for an hour, seeing, hearing, and feeling nothing of the bustle and jar of the streets, where they shall, in effect, find the city put far away from them. We want the greatest possible contrast with the streets and the shops and the rooms of the town which will be consistent with convenience and the preservation of good order and neatness. We want, especially, the greatest possible contrast with the restraining and confining conditions of the town, those conditions which compel us to walk circumspectly, watchfully, jealously, which compel us to look closely upon others without sympathy. Practically, what we most want is a simple, broad, open space of clean greensward, with sufficient play of surface and a sufficient number of trees about it to supply a variety of light and shade. This we want as a central feature. We want depth of wood enough about it not only for comfort in hot weather, but to completely shut out the city from our landscapes.

The word *park*, in town nomenclature, should, I think be reserved for grounds of the character and purpose thus described.

Not only as being the most valuable of all possible forms of public places, but regarded simply as a large space which will seriously interrupt cross-town communication wherever it occurs, the question of the site and bounds of

PAGE 137

a park requires to be determined with much more deliberation and art than is often secured for any problem of distant and extended municipal interests.

A Promenade may, with great advantage, be carried along the outer part of the surrounding groves of a park; and it will do no harm if here and there a broad opening among the trees discloses its open landscapes to those upon the promenade. But recollect that the object of the latter for the time being should be to see *congregated human life* under glorious and necessarily artificial conditions, and the natural landscape is not essential to them; though there is no more beautiful picture, and none can be more pleasing incidentally to the gregarious purpose, than that of beautiful meadows, over which clusters of level-armed sheltering trees cast broad shadows, and upon which are scattered dainty cows and flocks of black-faced sheep, while men, women, and children are seen sitting here and there forming groups in the shade, or moving in and out among the woody points and bays.

It may be inferred from what I have said, that very rugged ground, abrupt eminences, and what is technically called picturesque in distinction from merely beautiful or simply pleasing scenery, is not the most desirable for a town park. Decidedly not in my opinion. The park should, as far as possible, compliment the town. Openness is the one thing you cannot get in buildings. Picturesqueness you can get. Let your buildings be as picturesque as your artists can make them. This is the beauty of a town. Consequently, the beauty of the park should be the other. It should be the beauty of the fields, the meadow, the prairie, of the green pastures, and the still waters. What we want to gain is tranquility and rest to the mind. Mountains suggest effort. But besides this objection there are others of what I may indicate as the house-keeping class. It is impossible to give the public range over a large extent of ground of a highly picturesque character, unless under very exceptional circumstances, and sufficiently guard against the occurrence of opportunities and temptations to shabbiness, disorder, indecorum, and indecency, that will be subversive of every good purpose the park should be designed to fulfill.

PAGE 137

Nor can I think that in the park proper, what is called gardenesque beauty is to be courted; still less that highly artificial and exotic form of it, which, under the name of subtropical planting, the French have lately introduced, and in suitable positions with interesting and charming results, but in following which indiscreetly, the English are sacrificing the peculiar beauty of their simple and useful parks of the old time. Both these may have places, and very important places, but they do not belong within a park, unless as side scenes and incidents. Twenty years ago Hyde Park had a most pleasing, open, free, and inviting expression, though certainly it was too rude, too much wanting in art; but now art is vexed with long harsh lines of repellant iron-work, and here and there behind it bouquets of hot house plants, between which the public pass like hospital convalescents, who have been turned into the yard to walk about while their beds are making. We should undertake nothing in a park which involves the treating of the public as prisoners or wild beasts. A great object of all that is done in a park, of all the art of a park, is to influence the mind of men through their imagination, and the influence of iron hurdles can never be good.

PAGE 138

We have, perhaps, sufficiently defined the ideal of a park for a large town. It will seldom happen that this ideal can be realized fully. The next thing is to select the situation in which it can be most nearly approached without great cost; and by cost I do not mean simply cost of land or of construction, but cost of inconvenience and cost of keeping in order, which is a very much more serious matter, and should have a great deal more study.

A park fairly well managed near a large town, will surely become a new centre of that town. With the determination of location, size, and boundaries should therefore be associated the duty of arranging new trunk routes of communication between it and the distant parts of the town existing and forecasted.

These may be either narrow informal elongations of the park, varying say from two to five hundred feet in width, and radiating irregularly from it, or if, unfortunately, the town is already laid out in the unhappy way that New York and Brooklyn, San Francisco and Chicago, are, and, I am glad to say, Boston is not, on a plan made long years ago by a man who never saw a spring-carriage, and who had a conscientious dread of the Graces, then we must probably adopt formal parkways. They should be so planned and constructed as never to be noisy and seldom crowded, and so also that the straightforward movement of pleasure-carriages need never be obstructed, unless at absolutely necessary crossings, by slow-going heavy vehicles used for commercial purposes. If possible, also, they should be branched or reticulated with other ways of a similar class, so that no part of the town should finally be many minutes' walk from some one of them; and they should be made interesting by a process of planting and decoration, so that in necessarily passing through them, whether in going to or from the park, or to and from business, some substantial recreative advantage may be incidentally gained. It is a common error to regard a park as something to be produced complete in itself, as a picture to be painted on canvas. It should rather be planned as one to be done in fresco, with constant consideration of exterior objects, some of them quite at a distance and even existing as yet only in the imagination of the painter.

I have thus barely indicated a few of the points from which we may perceive our duty to apply the means in our hands to ends far distant, with reference to this problem of public recreations. Large operations of construction may not soon be desirable, but I hope you will agree with me that there is little room for question, that reserves of ground for the purposes I have referred to should be fixed upon as soon as possible, before the difficulty of arranging them, which arises from private building, shall be greatly more formidable than now....

It was frequently alleged [during the planning of Central Park], and with truth, that the use made of the existing public grounds was such as to develop riotous and licentious habits. A large park, it was argued, would inevitably present larger opportunities, and would be likely to exhibit an aggravated form of the same tendencies, consequently anything like refinement of treatment would be entirely wasted.

A few passages from a leading article of the *Herald* newspaper, in the seventh year of the enterprise, will indicate what estimate its astute editor had then formed of the prevailing convictions of the public on the subject:—"It is all folly to expect in this country to have parks like those in old aristocratic countries. When we open a public park Sam will air himself in it. He will take his friends whether from church, street, or elsewhere. He will knock down any better dressed man who remonstrates with him. He will talk and sing, and fill his share of the bench, and flirt with the nursery-maids in his own coarse way.

PAGE 138

Now we ask what chance have William B. Astor and Edward Everett against this fellow-citizen of theirs? Can they and he enjoy the same place? Is it not obvious that he will turn them out, and that the great Central Park will be nothing but a great bear-garden for the lowest denizens of the city, of which we shall yet pray litanies to be delivered."....

I have been asked if I supposed that "gentlemen" would ever resort to the Park, or would allow their wives and daughters to visit it? I heard a renowned lawyer argue that it was preposterous to suppose that a police force would do anything toward preserving order and decency in any broad piece of ground open to the general public of New York. And after the work began, I often heard the conviction expressed that if what was called the reckless, extravagant, inconsiderate policy of those who had the making of the Park in charge, could not be arrested, the weight of taxation and the general disgust which would be aroused among the wealthy classes would drive them from the city, and thus prove a serious injury to its prosperity.

"Why," said one, a man whom you all know by reputation, and many personally, "I should not ask for anything finer in my private grounds for the use of my own family." To whom it was replied that possibly grounds might not unwisely be prepared even more carefully when designed for the use of two hundred thousand families and their guests, than when designed for the use of one....

The question of the relative value of what is called off-hand common sense, and of special, deliberate, business-like study, must be settled in the case of the Central Park, by a comparison of benefit with cost. During the last four years over thirty million visits have been made to the Park by actual count, and many have passed uncounted. From fifty to eighty thousand persons on foot, thirty thousand in carriages, and four to five thousand on horseback, have frequently entered it in a day.

Among the frequent visitors, I have found all those who, a few years ago, believed it impossible that there should ever be a park in this republican country,—and especially in New York of all places in this country,—which would be a suitable place of resort for "gentlemen." They, their wives and daughters, frequent the Park more than they do the opera or the church.

There are many men of wealth who resort to the Park habitually and regularly, as much so as business men to their places of business. Of course, there is a reason for it, and a reason based upon their experience.

As to the effect on public health, there is no question that it is already great. The testimony of the older physicians of the city will be found unanimous on this point. Says one: "Where I formerly ordered patients of a certain class to give up their business altogether and go out of town, I now often advise simply moderation, and prescribe a ride in the Park before going to their offices, and again a drive with their families before dinner. By simply adopting this course as a habit, men who have been breaking down frequently recover tone rapidly, and are able to retain an active and controlling influence in an important business, from which they would have otherwise been forced to retire. I direct school-girls, under certain circumstances, to be taken wholly, or in part, from their studies, and sent to spend several hours a day rambling on foot in the Park."

The lives of women and children too poor to be sent to the country, can now be saved in thousands of instances, by making them go to the Park. During a hot day in July last, I counted at one time in the Park eighteen separate groups, consisting of mothers with their children, most of whom were under school-age, taking picnic dinners which they had brought from home with them. The practice is increasing under medical advice, especially when summer complaint is rife.

The much greater rapidity with which patients convalesce, and may be returned with safety to their ordinary occupations after severe illness, when they can be sent to the Park for a few hours a day, is beginning to be understood. The addition thus made to the productive labor of the city is not unimportant.

The Park, moreover, has had a very marked effect in making the city attractive to visitors, and in thus increasing its trade, and causing many who have made fortunes elsewhere to take up their residence and become tax-payers in it,—a much greater effect in this way, beyond all question, than all the colleges, schools, libraries, museums, and art-galleries which the city possesses. It has also induced many foreigners who have grown rich in the country, and who would otherwise have gone to Europe to enjoy their wealth,

PAGE 138–39

to settle permanently in the city. And what has become of the great Bugaboo? This is what the *Herald* of later date answers:—

PAGE 138–39

"When one is inclined to despair of the country, let him go to the Central Park on a Saturday, and spend a few hours there in looking at the people, not at those who come in gorgeous carriages, but at those who arrive on foot, or in those exceedingly democratic conveyances, the street-cars; and if, when the sun begins to sink behind the trees, he does not arise and go homeward with a happy swelling heart," and so on, the effusion winding up thus: "We regret to say that the more brilliant becomes the display of vehicles and toilettes, the more shameful is the display of bad manners on the part of the ----- extremely fine-looking people who ride in carriages and wear the fine dresses. We must add that the pedestrians always behave well."

CHAPTER 5

LANDSCAPE IS MORE THAN A LAWN

In Frederick Law Olmsted's writings about parks, one can hear the sweat beading on his brow. Olmsted, the landscape designer of Central and Prospect parks in New York City, the Emerald Necklace in Boston, the model suburb of Riverside (Illinois), and the Biltmore Estate in Asheville (North Carolina), essentially invented the American urban park in New York in 1857 with Central Park, and the profession of landscape architecture in the United States along with it. His style—the open greenswards bounded by thickets of trees, curving walks, rambles of greater "wildness," lakes like mirrors—developed in collaboration with partner Calvert Vaux, is now so familiar that these features have come to seem natural. Few users of his parks realize how little remains of the original landscape beneath and how much work has gone into making the hills roll and the trees shade. But the numbers do not lie: Central Park was built by a thousand workers (directed for a time by Olmsted as superintendent); five million cubic yards of stone, earth, and topsoil were moved into or out of the park; three hundred thousand trees and shrubs were planted. Construction took eighteen years, with the Civil War interrupting the work.

Olmsted's legacy is the willingness of municipalities to move stone, earth, and topsoil to make new landscapes, and an understanding of parks as an essential part of a healthy urban culture. The past decade has brought a resurgence of interest and investment in park making, the result of the population growth of many of the largest cities in the United States (particularly in terms of the numbers of families staying urban), the "discovery" of new land on former industrial, transportation, and utilities sites, and the increasing ambition of landscape architects in their role as place makers. Ada Louise Huxtable writes in "Down to Earth Masterpieces," her review of the 2005 Museum of Modern Art exhibition *Groundswell: Constructing the Contemporary Landscape*:

> In one of those totally unpredictable shifts in sensibility that occur when least expected, it is the landscape architects who are re-engaging today's radically innovative aesthetic with human needs and social functions; this is where the essential connections with the human condition are being made. And just in time, as architects, seduced by celebrity and technology, engaged in a dead-end contest in egos and engineering, have become more fixated on object making than place making, more removed from the intrinsic social purposes of their art.

In this brief paragraph Huxtable touches on a number of *themes* central to an understanding of the role of parks in cities and of the position of landscape architecture in the larger profession. But her themes closely parallel those raised by Olmsted when he wrote, in 1870, about the parks he was in the process of making. Like Louis Sullivan's "Tall Office Building Artistically Considered," Olmsted anatomizes the park from the inside out, identifying the basic structural elements that critics should still look for in the landscape. These enduring themes include the balance between architecture and landscape in the city, the socializing and democratizing influence of parks and play, parks as a recipe for health, and how and why we find room in the city for open space.

"Public Parks and the Enlargement of Towns," given as a speech and then disseminated as a book published by the American Social Science Association, is important as an early argument for parks as an essential element of and economic driver for the expanding American city. His focus is not on aesthetics or poetics, but on how the park works on mind and body. Given that most parks are publicly funded,

this broad-minded *approach* is key for the critic to keep in mind. The successful park cannot just be beautiful but must also be useful, and critical arguments for the success or failure of a park often turn to factors extrinsic to the design: place making as opposed to object making, in Huxtable's formulation.

This chapter explicates Olmsted's themes as background for the critic contemplating the contemporary park. It then offers an analysis of a recent criticism of New York City's High Line by *Metropolis* critic Karrie Jacobs that applies these ideas to a park radically different in style from Olmsted's lawns, promenades, and thickets.

Olmsted trained his eye during his travels, chronicled in *Walks and Talks of an American Farmer in England* (1850), *A Journey through Texas* (1857), and *The Cotton Kingdom* (1861). He saw landscapes in England as well as the western and southern United States, and combined descriptive writing with social commentary, observing people and places together. He also witnessed a changing United States, one moving from a rural, agricultural economy to an urban, industrial one. Cities were growing as grids of uninterrupted buildings, with few provisions for art, grace, or leisure. The streets needed civilization, and in the park Olmsted saw a way to offer some of the amenity he found in Europe.

The most direct inspiration for Central Park was found in Birkenhead Park, which opened in 1847 on the Wirral Peninsula opposite the city of Liverpool. Birkenhead was designed by Joseph Paxton, the self-taught gardener and landscape designer also responsible for another early modern masterpiece, the Crystal Palace exhibition hall of 1851. Birkenhead was the first park built on land purchased and maintained by a municipality, and was open to the entire public. Similar to earlier English parks of the period, it was also a real-estate venture, as house lots adjacent to Birkenhead were sold to members of the rising middle class. Olmsted visited in 1850, while working on *Walks and Talks*, and published an article on the park in Andrew Jackson Downing's the *Horticulturalist* in May 1851. His article discussed the simplicity of Birkenhead's landscape, its public financing, and its popularity across classes.

By 1870 Olmsted was transformed from observer to maker, and his discussion of public parks treats them as tools. The first and most important quality of the city park is its difference from the town, as the park must serve as antidote to the density and commercial activity of the city. He writes, "We want a ground to which people may easily go after their day's work is done, and where they may stroll for an hour, seeing, hearing, and feeling nothing of the bustle and jar of the streets, where they shall, in effect, find the city put far away from them....[The beauty of the park] should be the beauty of the fields, the meadow, the prairie, of the green pastures, and the still waters." His language is unusually poetic in both these cases, as he strives to emphasize the difference, and the purpose of that difference, between park and town. He has already described, in sociological terms, the unhealthy nature of most living and working conditions in the late nineteenth-century city, and his descriptions of park are intended as contrasts. *Openness, tranquility, strolling, stillness.*

In the paragraphs in which he describes the ideal park, Olmsted links design to its effects, not assuming that his listeners will have the same associations with lawns, mountains, or promenades as he does. This connection between the visual and the physical is always one of the trickiest for critics to make but is essential in allowing the reader to "see" through your eyes. He is showing, not telling, why the parks he has made work for the city.

Greensward was Olmsted's first name for Central Park, and it is there and at Brooklyn's Prospect Park that the "simple, broad, open space" he describes can be seen in three dimensions. The impression of nature on the Sheep Meadow in Central Park can be almost absolute; surrounding buildings disappear behind banks of trees. Olmsted imagined groups of people strolling, picnicking, traveling in groups. Those movements were also part of his plan, as they contrasted in speed and the level of social interaction with what was happening on city streets. He writes that only in his parks, will you "find a body of Christians coming together, and with an evident glee in the prospect of coming together, all classes largely represented, with a common purpose, not at all intellectual, competitive with none, disposing to jealousy and spiritual or intellectual pride toward none, each individual adding by his mere presence to the pleasure of all others, all helping to the greater happiness of each."

This is his second theme: the civilizing influence of the park. Only in the park could people of different classes and races indulge in a common, free activity, seeing each others' manners on equal footing. For this to occur, the park needed to be relatively unprogrammed, without paid activities or grounds set aside for specific sports. The workday and the weekday were slaves to time; the weekend, spent in the park, was a time for picnics and people watching. That this was a controversial position is evident in the latter part of the speech, where he mentions the fears of "gentlemen" that the park will be too dangerous for their wives and daughters, and niceties of design wasted on "Sam."

Olmsted realized, long before multiday outdoor music festivals, the joy of the crowd. An empty park is dangerous, and it is also not fun. The mixing of classes, religions, and ages was part of the attraction, another aspect of the scenery. In Jane Jacobs's *The Death and Life of Great American Cities*, she discusses the importance of people to parks: users that occupy the park at different times of day, parks big enough to accommodate different levels of activity and exertion. There is safety in diversity. Olmsted quotes the *Herald*, coming to the same realization:

> When one is inclined to despair of the country, let him go to the Central Park on a Saturday, and spend a few hours there in looking at the people, not at those who come in gorgeous carriages, but at those who arrive on foot, or in those exceedingly democratic conveyances, the street-cars; and if, when the sun begins to sink behind the trees, he does not arise and go homeward with a happy swelling heart.

A series of design choices connects the intellectual idea of open, transparent, democratic space to the physical realm. These choices range from broad strokes like the porosity between the different outdoor "rooms" of Central Park (one can usually see another kind of landscape from the one being occupied, such as open spaces from wooded paths, sunlit lawns from shady groves), to small things like the absence of fences, gates, and other ironwork. This last physical choice was made for a specific behavioral reason, as Olmsted writes, "We should undertake nothing in a park which involves the treating of the public as prisoners or wild beasts." A wall to clearly define the outside was fine, but inside only natural slopes and rocky barriers should separate one zone from the next. In Central Park, for example, the east–west roads are even sunken below the landscape so as not to carve the park visually into five rectangular sections.

Olmsted's third theme is health. One of his primary economic arguments for the benefits of parks is the increase in productivity that comes from a healthier populace. The park, by providing free recreation and greenery, offers a tonic to the overtaxed urban working class. Olmsted places particular stress, in his discussion of the health benefits of parks, on the tree. Trees planted along the streets were a blessing too rarely bestowed, he writes, but their placement close to the busy roads was often bad for the trees. Trees in a park had room to flourish and, despite their distance from some parts of town, would purify the air of an overbuilt city, increasing the health of the population and reducing the incidence of disease. Planners today still envision trees in the same first-responder role: one of the catchiest items in PlaNYC, a 2007 blueprint for the sustainable growth of New York City, was MillionTreesNYC, an initiative to plant one million trees along streets, in parks, and on private property in ten years. By 2010 the city was halfway to the goal. Olmsted quotes physicians as prescribing visits to Central Park for working men and schoolgirls alike, the rest and clean air restoring them to health without leaving the boundaries of the city.

Olmsted's final theme is growth (how and why urban leaders and planners need to make room for parks). He appeals to civic and social ideals—democracy, public health, economic benefit—suggesting that the future success of cities lies in parks. Rather than driving the upper classes away with taxation, Central Park, "has had a very marked effect in making the city attractive to visitors, and in thus increasing its trade, and causing many who have made fortunes elsewhere to take up their residence and become tax-payers in it,—a much greater effect in this way, beyond all question, than all the colleges, schools, libraries, museums, and art-galleries which the city possesses."

This argument, which can be seen as integral to the growth and success of Olmsted's business, ultimately influenced the placement of his parks. In New York, both Central and Prospect parks were carved out of grids laid over land that was still preurban. "Central" was a prediction of things to come in Manhattan. (Thinking about the origins of Central Park always reminds me of a telling aside in Edith Wharton's *The Age of Innocence*, in which Mrs. Manson Mingott has "put the crowning touch to her audacities by building a large house of pale cream-colored stone [what came to be called brownstone was de rigeur] in an inaccessible wilderness near the Central Park.")

In other cities, already more closely built, Olmsted had to take what he could get. For example, in Boston the so-called Emerald Necklace, a set of linear parks linked by waterways, ends in the large-scale Franklin Park but wends its way through the city in a series of smaller ribbons of green along existing wetlands called the Fens. Riverside and Morningside parks in New York make use of their hilly sites and edge conditions: the former to screen the houses on Riverside Drive from the less-than-picturesque railroad tracks, the latter to ease the change in grade between central Harlem and Morningside Heights. In each case the no-man's land adjacent to the park soon filled in with expensive building, increasing real-estate value for private owners after vast public expenditure.

Olmsted's pragmatic approach, and emphasis on economic and democratic themes, can be seen today in the work of critic Karrie Jacobs. Jacobs writes the monthly America column for *Metropolis* magazine and has also been architecture critic for *New York* magazine, founding editor of *Dwell* magazine, and author of the 2006 book *The Perfect $100,000 House: A Trip Across America and Back in Pursuit of a Place to Call Home*. Her *Metropolis* column focuses on architecture and design in the American landscape, often featuring small-scale projects and observations based on living with design rather than reviews of new buildings by famous architects. Her typically skeptical approach was applied in her June 2009 column, "Beyond the Hype," to the High Line park, recently completed on the west side of Manhattan:

> How many articles have you read about the High Line in the decade since Joshua David and Robert Hammond began their unlikely quest to rescue an elevated freight line running along the West Side of Manhattan? There were endless stories about the original preservation battle, illustrated by those glorious Joel Sternfeld photos of New York's secret meadow. In 2004, when Friends of the High Line, the organization founded by David and Hammond, held a design competition (won by

Field Operations and Diller Scofidio + Renfro), the renderings were everywhere. And there have been plenty of pieces, in this magazine and others, that focused on the leadership role of the landscape-architecture firm Field Operations and its principal, James Corner. Has a project ever been more hyped?

I always wanted the High Line to be preserved, but I also wanted it to be left alone. I thought—and still think—it was sad that Manhattan had been developed to the point where there was no room or tolerance for decay (at least aboveground; the subway system is another matter). I've occasionally thought of the High Line as a symbol of an overheated design culture that shuns the ordinary or the unstylish.

Jacobs, like Olmsted, doesn't want to talk about style. She wants to talk about how the High Line happened and what's happening around it. Her interest as a critic is typically in the larger message of a building that works or a project that fails. It is replicability, the idea of a park as a repeatable, sensible urban amenity, that she wants to be her theme.

The High Line initially turned her off because it seemed like a one-off, too expensive and specific in its design to be a model. As a park the High Line would seem to be Olmsted's nightmare. Long and narrow, there is no room for a lawn. Elevated and artificially filled, the soil is too shallow for big trees. The city presses in, sometimes closely as the railroad trestle on which it is built goes through several buildings. The extreme narrowness of the trestle makes it impossible to ignore the design choices of the project lead, James Corner Field Operations (with architects Diller Scofidio + Renfro [DS+R]), planting specialist Piet Oudolf, and lighting designers L'Observatoire), because there's nowhere to get lost in nature. Olmsted's first theme, that the park be an antidote to the city, seems impossible to realize, as the buildings can never be blotted out as they are in Central or Prospect parks. But Jacobs saw the new architecture rising around the High Line as a form of foliage:

> The height, about three stories up, is just enough to alter your point of view. It's voyeur height rather than spectacle height. It immerses you in the city instead of elevating you above it....

…From here, you'll be able to see New York's most convincing 21st-century cityscapes. At the southern end of the High Line, on Gansevoort Street just west of Washington, an old meatpacking plant is being demolished to make way for the Whitney Museum of American Art's downtown branch.…Immediately north is the newly opened Standard Hotel. A skinny lozenge on piers that straddles the High Line, it's surely the best thing that has ever emerged from Polshek Partnership. At the north end of the section that will open in June… is the most remarkable cluster of new buildings in New York: Frank Gehry's distinctive IAC headquarters…Jean Nouvel's Eleventh Avenue condo tower, clad in a glass mosaic textured like lizard skin; Shigeru Ban's condos, with exterior walls formed by rolling metal shutters; and a tidy green-glass condo designed by Annabelle Selldorf. Immediately to the east, you see the skinny frame of Neil Denari's first building, HL23, poking up behind a billboard. Is the High Line responsible for this creative efflorescence? Maybe not entirely, but it certainly seems to figure prominently in the imaginations of those who finance and market condos.

The city does not disappear but is transformed, making a stroll on the High Line indeed different from the bustling sidewalks below. Jacobs does not refer to Olmsted explicitly, but the idea of the urban park created by Olmsted is the background for her discussion. By recognizing the new architecture as scenery, Jacobs also conflates two of Olmsted's themes: the park as an antidote and the park as an economic generator. The buildings she describes are the modern-day equivalent of the famous Dakota apartment house, built opposite Central Park when the west side was rural, or Mrs. Manson Mingott's east side mansion from *The Age of Innocence*. Developers speculating on the success of the park built new residences nearby while the High Line itself was still under construction.

Jacobs, like Olmsted, allows herself only a few moments of poetic appreciation. The *organization* of her review is the classic walking tour, the reader following along as David leads her: "I followed David…who pointed out the skinny baby trees of the 'Gansevoort Woodlands' and the pink and yellow blossoms sprouting from mulch near the 'Sundeck Preserve.' The High Line's place names seem to come from the realm of boyish fantasy games, but the landscape itself is wonderfully restrained, a mannered but heartfelt homage to the wild growth of the rail line's period of abandonment." She rolls her eyes, metaphorically speaking, at the pastoral place names given to sections of the trestle. Like the "overheated design culture" that spawned the High Line and its surrounding buildings, the names seem to her to be a little too much, indications that the High Line can only happen here in Chelsea, a neighborhood of art galleries and designer clothing shops.

By the end of her review, the tour has convinced her that the High Line can mean something universal for the enlargement of towns. The walking tour parallels a mental tour, and what seems to be a straightforward narrative becomes a critical one. Jacobs never takes up Olmsted's theme of health (perhaps because the idea that green space makes a better city now goes without saying), but she concludes with a contemporary version of the search for places where city and park might grow up together. Rather than being an elitist playground, making the High Line into a public park has attracted more people (and more people of different backgrounds) to this section of the city. The style design does not overpower or repel, but serves appropriately as a backdrop for the new cityscape and the kind of people watching Olmsted preferred. Unexpectedly, her theme cleaves to that of Charles Moore in "You Have to Pay for the Public Life." Park, monument, and infrastructure can often be the same thing, if you know how and where to look. For Jacobs, the High Line "suggests unlimited opportunities for transforming eyesores into assets, for radical adaptive reuse." She continues:

> Surely, in the rail line's heyday we didn't know that at some point we'd no longer need freight trains to supply the city's West Side factories with raw ingredients—or that someday we wouldn't even need the factories themselves. Similarly, right now we can't imagine that one day we might no longer have a use for the elevated expressways that bisect our neighborhoods....
>
> ...The High Line outperforms its hype because it says something simple and profound: Anything is possible.

When Olmsted began designing urban parks in the 1850s, the form of his parks seemed as strange as the High Line's did in the early 2000s. The questions asked of their planners, boosters, and designers must have been the same: You want to put a park where? Who will come? Will it be safe? Will it be a burden to taxpayers? Why a park when you might have more buildings? But Olmsted saw, as High Line founders David and Hammond would more than one hundred years later, that a park was much more than an open space with plants. He crafted a series of economic, pragmatic, medical, and social rationales for why America's growing cities needed parks and presented them in "Public Parks and the Enlargement of Towns."

His themes resonate today, and his antistylistic arguments form a template for contemporary critique of landscape architecture. Huxtable, in her review of a museum exhibit of new parks, and Jacobs, in her review of the High Line, stress almost everything but the design in evaluating the lessons to be learned from landscape, rapping architects on the knuckles for excessive form making. The leap Jacobs makes from the High Line at the end of her review, that this park proves anything is possible, is not so far from Olmsted's position in the 1870s.

Central Park seems entirely natural to us now, but its creation required as much imagination in its day as building the High Line park on a railroad trestle did in the present. Both projects required placing the public good before private enterprise, but both subsequently created a real-estate gold rush. Writing about parks means writing about the city that surrounds them, which Jacobs makes explicit in her description of the new buildings defining the trestle's negative space. What has changed, and is still changing, is what constitutes an escape from the urban daily grind, and it is up to the critic to see foliage in new places.

CHECKLIST

In Olmsted's 1870 speech, he identifies a number of the urban roles the parks can play. Choose a park in your city or town and interrogate it. How does it fulfill (or not) the following functions?

1. As an antidote to the city: "The idea of the park itself must always be uppermost in the eye of the beholder."

2. As a democratizing force: What physical aspects of the park (in your observation) create new opportunities for social interaction?

3. As an air purifier: How green do parks need to be? Is grass necessary? Chairs? Open space?

4. As a developer: Where could a park best be built in your city? How would it alter its shape and focus?

5. Jacobs questions the need for elaborate contemporary design at the High Line. Can design get in the way in a park? Compare an old park and a newer one, looking at design elements like benches, lighting, plantings, paths. Which is more popular? Which is more comfortable?

The Death and Life of Great American Cities

JANE JACOBS

———

Originally published 1961 by Random House

Part One: Chapter 2
The uses of sidewalks: safety

…A city street equipped to handle strangers, and to make a safety asset, in itself, out of the presence of strangers, as the streets of successful city neighborhoods always do, must have three main qualities:

First, there must be a clear demarcation between what is public space and what is private space. Public and private spaces cannot ooze into each other as they do typically in suburban settings or in projects.

Second, there must be eyes upon the street, eyes belonging to those we might call the natural proprietors of the street. The buildings on a street equipped to handle strangers and to insure the safety of both residents and strangers, must be oriented to the street. They cannot turn their backs or blank sides on it and leave it blind.

And third, the sidewalk must have users on it fairly continuously, both to add to the number of effective eyes on the street and to induce the people in buildings along the street to watch the sidewalks in sufficient numbers. Nobody enjoys sitting on a stoop or looking out a window at an empty street. Almost nobody does such a thing. Large numbers of people entertain themselves, off and on, by watching street activity.

PAGE 162

In settlements that are smaller and simpler than big cities, controls on acceptable public behavior, if not on crime, seem to operate with greater or lesser success through a web of reputation, gossip, approval, disapproval and sanctions, all of which are powerful if people know each other and word travels. But a city's streets, which must control not only the behavior of the people of the city but also of visitors from suburbs and towns who want to have a big time away from the gossip and sanctions at home, have to operate by more direct, straightforward methods. It is a wonder cities have solved such an inherently difficult problem at all. And yet in many streets they do it magnificently....

Under the seeming disorder of the old city, wherever the old city is working successfully, is a marvelous order for maintaining the safety of the streets and the freedom of the city. It is a complex order. Its essence is intricacy of sidewalk use, bringing with it a constant succession of eyes. This order is all composed of movement and change, and although it is life, not art, we may fancifully call it the art form of the city and liken it to the dance—not to a simple-minded precision dance with everyone kicking up at the same time, twirling in unison and bowing off en masse, but to an intricate ballet in which the individual dancers and ensembles all have distinctive parts which miraculously reinforce each other and compose an orderly whole. The ballet of the good city sidewalk never repeats itself from place to place, and in any one place is always replete with new improvisations.

The stretch of Hudson Street where I live is each day the scene of an intricate sidewalk ballet. I make my own first entrance into it a little after eight when I put out the garbage can, surely a prosaic occupation, but I enjoy my part, my little clang, as the droves of junior high school students walk by the center of the stage dropping candy wrappers. (How do they eat so much candy so early in the morning?)

PAGE 162

While I sweep up the wrappers I watch the other rituals of morning: Mr. Halpert unlocking the laundry's handcart from its mooring to a cellar door, Joe Cornacchia's son-in-law stacking out the empty crates from the delicatessen, the barber bringing out his sidewalk folding chair, Mr. Goldstein arranging the coils of wire which proclaim the hardware store is open, the wife of the tenement's superintendent depositing her chunky three-year-old with a toy mandolin on the stoop, the vantage point from which he is learning the English his mother cannot speak. Now the primary children, heading for St. Luke's, dribble through to the south; the children for St. Veronica's cross, heading to the west, and the children for P.S. 41, heading toward the cast. Two new entrances are being made from the wings: well-dressed and even elegant women and men with brief cases emerge from doorways and side streets. Most of these are heading for the bus and subways, but some hover on the curbs, stopping taxis which have miraculously appeared at the right moment, for the taxis are part of a wider morning ritual: having dropped passengers from midtown in the downtown financial district, they are now bringing downtowners up to midtown. Simultaneously, numbers of women in housedresses have emerged and as they crisscross with one another they pause for quick conversations that sound with either laughter or joint indignation, never, it seems, anything between. It is time for me to hurry to work too, and I exchange my ritual farewell with Mr. Lofaro, the short, thick-bodied, white-aproned fruit man who stands outside his doorway a little up the street, his arms folded, his feet planted, looking solid as earth itself. We nod; we each glance quickly up and down the street, then look back to each other and smile. We have done this many a morning for more than ten years, and we both know what it means: All is well.

The heart-of-the-day ballet I seldom see, because part of the nature of it is that working people who live there, like me, are mostly gone, filling the roles of strangers on other sidewalks. But from days off, I know enough of it to know that it becomes more and more intricate. Longshoremen who are not working that day gather at the White Horse or the Ideal or the International for beer and conversation. The executives and business lunchers from the industries just to the west throng the Dorgene restaurant and the Lion's Head coffee house; meat-market workers and communications scientists fill the bakery lunchroom. Character dancers come on, a strange old man with strings of old shoes over his shoulders, motor-scooter riders with big beards and girl friends who bounce on the back of the scooters and wear their hair long in front of their faces as well as behind, drunks who follow the advice of the Hat Council and are always turned out in hats, but not hats the Council would approve. Mr. Lacey, the locksmith, shuts up his shop for a while and goes to exchange the time of day with Mr. Slube at the cigar store. Mr. Koochagian, the tailor, waters the luxuriant jungle of plants in his window, gives them a critical look from the outside, accepts a compliment on them from two passers-by, fingers the leaves on the plane tree in front of our house with a thoughtful gardener's appraisal, and crosses the street for a bite at the Ideal where he can keep an eye on customers and wigwag across the message that he is coming. The baby carriages come out, and clusters of everyone from toddlers with dolls to teen-agers with homework gather at the stoops.

When I get home after work, the ballet is reaching its crescendo. This is the time of roller skates and stilts and tricycles, and games in the lee of the stoop with bottletops and plastic cowboys; this is the time of bundles and packages, zigzagging from the drug store to the fruit stand and back over to the butcher's; this is the time when teen-agers, all dressed up, are pausing to ask if their slips show or their collars look right; this is the time when beautiful girls get out of MG's; this is the time when the fire engines go through; this is the time when anybody you know around Hudson Street will go by.

As darkness thickens and Mr. Halpert moors the laundry cart to the cellar door again, the ballet goes on under lights, eddying back and forth but intensifying at the bright spotlight pools of Joe's sidewalk pizza dispensary, the bars, the delicatessen, the restaurant and the drug store. The night workers stop now at the delicatessen, to pick up salami and a container of milk. Things have settled down for the evening but the street and its ballet have not come to a stop.

I know the deep night ballet and its seasons best from waking long after midnight to tend a baby and, sitting in the dark, seeing the shadows and hearing the sounds of the sidewalk. Mostly it is a sound like infinitely pattering snatches of party conversation and, about three in the morning, singing, very good singing. Sometimes there is sharpness and anger or sad, sad weeping, or a flurry of search for a string of beads broken. One night a young man came roaring along, bellowing terrible language at two girls whom he had apparently picked up and who were disappointing him. Doors opened, a wary semicircle formed around him, not too close, until the police came. Out came the heads, too, along Hudson Street, offering opinion, "Drunk…Crazy…A wild kid from the suburbs."

Deep in the night, I am almost unaware how many people are on the street unless something calls them together, like the bagpipe. Who the piper was and why he favored our street I have no idea. The bagpipe just skirled out in the February night, and as if it were a signal the random, dwindled movements of the sidewalk took on direction. Swiftly, quietly, almost magically a little crowd was there, a crowd that evolved into a circle with a Highland fling inside it. The crowd could be seen on the shadowy sidewalk, the dancers could be seen, but the bagpiper himself was almost invisible because his bravura was all in his music. He was a very little man in a plain brown overcoat. When he finished and vanished, the dancers and watchers applauded, and applause came from the galleries too, half a dozen of the hundred windows on Hudson Street. Then the windows closed, and the little crowd dissolved into the random movements of the night street.

The strangers on Hudson Street, the allies whose eyes help us natives keep the peace of the street, are so many they always seem to be different people from one day to the next. That does not matter. Whether they are so many always-different people as they seem to be, I do not know. Likely they are. When Jimmy Rogan fell through a plate-glass window (he was separating some scuffling friends) and almost lost his arm, a stranger in an old T shirt emerged from the Ideal bar, swiftly applied an expert tourniquet and, according to the hospital's emergency staff, saved Jimmy's life. Nobody remembered seeing the man before and no one has seen him since. The hospital was called in this way: a woman sitting on the steps next to the accident ran over to the bus stop, wordlessly snatched the dime from the hand of a stranger who was waiting with his fifteen-cent fare ready, and raced into the Ideal's phone booth. The stranger raced after her to offer the nickel too. Nobody remembered seeing him before, and no one has seen him since.

When you see the same stranger three or four times on Hudson Street, you begin to nod. This is almost getting to be an acquaintance, a public acquaintance, of course.

I have made the daily ballet of Hudson Street sound more frenetic than it is, because writing it telescopes it. In real life, it is not that way. In real life, to be sure, something is always going on, the ballet is never at a halt, but the general effect is peaceful and the general tenor even leisurely. People who know well such animated city streets will know how it is. I am afraid people who do not will always have it a little wrong in their heads—like the old prints of rhinoceroses made from travelers' descriptions of rhinoceroses.

On Hudson Street, the same as in the North End of Boston or in any other animated neighborhoods of great cities, we are not innately more competent at keeping the sidewalks safe than are the people who try to live off the hostile truce of Turf in a blind-eyed city. We are the lucky possessors of a city order that makes it relatively simple to keep the peace because there are plenty of eyes on the street. But there is nothing simple about that order itself, or the bewildering number of components that go into it. Most of those components are specialized in one way or another. They unite in their joint effect upon the sidewalk, which is not specialized in the least. That is its strength.

PAGE 162

Part Two: Chapter 8
The need for primary mixed uses

> Condition 1: *The district, and indeed as many of its internal parts as possible, must serve more than one primary function; preferably more than two. These must insure the presence of people who go outdoors on different schedules and are in the place for different purposes, but who are able to use many facilities in common.*

On successful city streets, people must appear at different times. This is time considered on a small scale, hour by hour through the day. I have

PAGE 164

already explained this necessity in social terms while discussing street safety and also neighborhood parks. Now I shall point out its economic effects.

Neighborhood parks, you will recall, need people who are in the immediate vicinity for different purposes from one another, or else the parks will be used only sporadically.

PAGE 164

Most consumer enterprises are just as dependent as parks on people going to and fro throughout the day, but with this difference: If parks lie idle, it is bad for them and their neighborhoods but they do not disappear as a consequence. If consumer enterprises lie idle for much of the day they may disappear. Or, to be more accurate, in most such cases they never appear in the first place. Stores, like parks, need users.

For a humble example of the economic effects of people spread through time of day, I will ask you to think back to a city sidewalk scene: the ballet of Hudson Street. The continuity of this movement (which gives the street its safety) depends on an economic foundation of basic mixed uses. The workers from the laboratories, meat-packing plants, warehouses, plus those from a bewildering variety of small manufacturers, printers and other little industries and offices, give all the eating places and much of the other commerce support at midday. We residents on the street and on its more purely residential tributaries could and would support a modicum of commerce by ourselves, but relatively little. We possess more convenience, liveliness, variety and choice than we "deserve" in our own right. The people who work in the neighborhood also possess, on account of us residents, more variety than they "deserve" in their own right. We support these things together by unconsciously cooperating economically. If the neighborhood were to lose the industries, it would be a disaster for us residents. Many enterprises, unable to exist on residential trade by itself, would disappear. Or if the industries were to lose us residents, enterprises unable to exist on the working people by themselves would disappear.

As it is, workers and residents together are able to produce more than the sum of our two parts. The enterprises we are capable of supporting, mutually, draw out onto the sidewalk by evening many more residents than would emerge if the place were moribund. And, in a modest way, they also attract still another crowd in addition to the local residents or local workers. They attract people who want a change from their neighborhoods, just as we frequently want a change from ours. This attraction exposes our commerce to a still larger and more diverse population, and this in turn has permitted a still further growth and range of commerce living on all three kinds of population in varying proportions: a shop down the street selling prints, a store that rents diving equipment, a dispensary of first-rate pizza, a pleasant coffee house.

Sheer numbers of people using city streets, and the way those people are spread through the hours of the day, are two different matters. I shall deal with sheer numbers in another chapter; at this stage it is important to understand that numbers, in themselves, are not an equivalent for people distributed through time of day.

Part Two: Chapter 9
The need for small blocks

…Nor do long blocks possess more virtue in other cities than they do in New York. In Philadelphia there is a neighborhood in which buildings are simply being let fall down by their owners, in an area between the downtown and the city's major belt of public housing projects. There are many reasons for this neighborhood's hopelessness, including the nearness of the rebuilt city with its social disintegration and danger, but obviously the neighborhood has not been helped by its own physical structure. The standard Philadelphia block is 400 feet square (halved by the alleys-become-streets where the city is most successful). In this falling-down neighborhood some of that "street waste" was eliminated in the original street layout; some of its blocks are 700 feet long. It stagnated, of course, beginning from the time it was built up. In Boston, the North End, which is a marvel of "wasteful" streets and fluidity of cross-use, has been heroically unslumming itself against official apathy and financial opposition.

The myth that plentiful city streets are "wasteful," one of the verities of orthodox planning, comes of course from the Garden City and Radiant City theorists who decried the use of land for streets because they wanted that land consolidated instead into project prairies. This myth is especially destructive because it interferes intellectually with our ability to see one of the simplest, most unnecessary, and most easily corrected reasons for much stagnation and failure.

Super-block projects are apt to have all the disabilities of long blocks, frequently in exaggerated form, and this is true even when they are laced with promenades and malls, and thus, in theory, possess streets at reasonable intervals through which people can make their way. These streets are meaningless because there is, seldom any active reason for a good cross-section of people to use them. Even in passive terms, simply as various alternative changes of scene in getting from here to yonder, these paths are meaningless because all their scenes are essentially the same. The situation is the opposite from that the New Yorker reporter noticed in the blocks between Fifth and Sixth avenues. There people try to hunt out streets which they need but which are missing. In projects, people are apt to avoid malls and cross-malls which are there, but are pointless.

I bring up this problem not merely to berate the anomalies of project planning again, but to indicate that frequent streets and short blocks are valuable because of the fabric of intricate cross-use that they permit among the users of a city neighborhood. Frequent streets are not an end in themselves. They are a means toward an end. If that end—generating diversity and catalyzing the plans of many people besides planners—is thwarted by too repressive zoning, or by regimented construction that precludes the flexible growth of diversity, nothing significant can be accomplished by short blocks. Like mixtures of primary use, frequent streets are effective in helping to generate diversity only because of the way they perform. The means by which they work (attracting mixtures of users along them) and the results they can help accomplish (the growth of diversity) are inextricably related. The relationship is reciprocal.

PAGE 168–69

Part Two: Chapter 10
The need for aged buildings

Condition 3: *The district must mingle buildings that vary in age and condition, including a good proportion of old ones.*

Cities need old buildings so badly it is probably impossible for vigorous streets and districts to grow without them. By old buildings I mean not museum-piece old buildings, not old buildings in an excellent and expensive state of rehabilitation—although these make fine ingredients—but also a good lot of plain, ordinary, low-value old buildings, including some rundown old buildings.

If a city area has only new buildings, the enterprises that can exist there are automatically limited to those that can support the high costs of new construction. These high costs of occupying new buildings may be levied in the form of rent, or they may be levied in the form of an owner's interest and amortization payments on the capital costs of the construction. However the costs are paid off, they have to be paid off. And for this reason, enterprises that support the cost of new construction must be capable of paying a relatively high overhead—high in comparison to that necessarily required by old buildings. To support such high overheads, the enterprises must be either (a) high profit or (b) well subsidized.

If you look about, you will see that only operations that are well established, high-turnover, standardized or heavily subsidized can afford, commonly, to carry the costs of new construction. Chain stores, chain restaurants and banks go into new construction. But neighborhood bars, foreign restaurants and pawn shops go into older buildings. Supermarkets and shoe stores often go into new buildings; good bookstores and antique dealers seldom do. Well-subsidized opera and art museums often go into new buildings. But the unformalized feeders of the arts—studios, galleries, stores for musical instruments and art supplies, backrooms where the low earning power of a scat and a table can absorb uneconomic discussions—these go into old buildings. Perhaps more significant, hundreds of ordinary enterprises, necessary to the safety and public life of streets and neighborhoods, and appreciated for their convenience and personal quality, can make out successfully in old buildings, but are inexorably slain by the high overhead of new construction.

As for really new ideas of any kind—no matter how ultimately profitable or otherwise successful some of them might prove to be—there is no leeway for such chancy trial, error and experimentation in the high-overhead economy of new construction. Old ideas can sometimes use new buildings. New ideas must use old buildings.

PAGE 169

Even the enterprises that can support new construction in cities need old construction in their immediate vicinity. Otherwise they are part of a total attraction and total environment that is economically too limited—and therefore functionally too limited to be lively, interesting and convenient. Flourishing diversity anywhere in a city means the mingling of high-yield, middling-yield, low-yield and no-yield enterprises.

The only harm of aged buildings to a city district or street is the harm that eventually comes of nothing but old age—the harm that lies in everything being old and everything becoming worn out. But a city area in such a situation is not a failure because of being all old. It is the other way around. The area is all old because it is a failure. For some other reason or combination of reasons, all its enterprises or people are unable to support new construction. It has, perhaps, failed to hang on to its own people or enterprises that do become successful enough to support new building or rehabilitation; they leave when they become this successful. It has also failed to attract newcomers with choice; they see no opportunities or attractions here. And in some cases, such an area may be so infertile economically that enterprises which might grow into successes in other places, and build or rebuild their shelter, never make enough money in this place to do so.

A successful city district becomes a kind of ever-normal granary so far as construction is concerned. Some of the old buildings, year by year, are replaced by new ones—or rehabilitated to a degree equivalent to replacement. Over the years there is, therefore, constantly a mixture of buildings of many ages and types. This is, of course, a dynamic process, with what was once new in the mixture eventually becoming what is old in the mixture.

We are dealing here again, as we were in the case of mixed primary uses, with the economic effects of time. But in this case we are dealing with the economics of time not hour by hour through the day, but with the economics of time by decades and generations.

Time makes the high building costs of one generation the bargains of a following generation. Time pays off original capital costs, and this depreciation can be reflected in the yields required from a building. Time makes certain structures obsolete for some enterprises, and they become available to others. Time can make the space efficiencies of one generation the space luxuries of another generation. One century's building commonplace is another century's useful aberration.

CHAPTER 6

CRITICISM FROM THE GROUND UP

Jane Jacobs was among the most influential citizen critics of the past century. Her first book, *The Death and Life of Great American Cities* (1961), still casts a long shadow over planning professionals (whom she often dismissed) and public advocates (whom she typically championed). Turns of phrase she used in the book are today parroted by architects, critics, and city planners, and even incorporated into new zoning regulations. When Amanda Burden, current director of the New York City Department of City Planning, insists on street-level shops for new development projects in the Williamsburg neighborhood of Brooklyn, she is quoting Jacobs (specifically, part one, chapter 2, "The Uses of Sidewalks: Safety," from *Death and Life*). When Herbert Muschamp writes in "The Miracle in Bilbao" of the transformative power of artists on industrial cities, he is quoting Jacobs (part two, chapter 10, "The Need for Aged Buildings"). When the site plan for Ground Zero reopens Greenwich Street as a north-south artery, the Manhattan street grid is quoting Jacobs (part two, chapter 9, "The Need for Small Blocks").

Jacobs learned not from books but from her experiences as a New Yorker, a journalist, and a mother living in the West Village during the postwar years. Her analysis was inductive, based on inhabiting her space, and it was from living, working, and watching city life that she built an urban theory. The best-known selections from *Death and Life* are the initial chapters that focus on Jacobs's own low-rise neighborhood as a sort of ideal urban organism. These chapters are a means of telling you where she is coming from, a prelude to the grander, integrated set of "needs" presented in part two, "The Conditions for City Diversity." These needs include "primary mixed uses," "small blocks," "aged buildings," "concentration."

Part one, "The Peculiar Nature of Cities," is instructive for its method—the closeness of her observation, her integration of architectural, social, and experiential anecdotes—but ultimately too restricted to the low-rise row-house-neighborhood experience to be widely applicable to other places. Based on this first section, set among brownstones and corner stores, it is possible to dismiss Jacobs as sentimental, even conservative, when she wanted to be thought of as the first urban ecologist. Jacobs's vision isn't universally applicable, because it is, in her first book, so based on personal experience. But that doesn't mean she hasn't rigorously examined her specific sphere. Her anecdotes are not without purpose, and their accessibility offers a way to talk about cities that any critic would do well to consider.

Too often, writing about cities takes a bird's-eye view, which can be alienating and disorienting for those more accustomed to walking. The excerpt reprinted on the preceding pages includes her famous description of Hudson Street's "sidewalk ballet," but the majority of the reprint is from part two, for it is with the ideas presented there that the critic can start to imagine what a new Jacobsian city would look like and to apply her theory to present-day projects.

This chapter is divided into two parts. The first describes Jacobs's method and explicates key enduring arguments about what cities need. The second considers a recent urban-planning controversy in Brooklyn over the design and development of the set of Metropolitan Transportation Authority rail yards known as Atlantic Yards. The critique of this project serve as an opportunity to apply Jacobs to the contemporary city, showing how writers like Paul Goldberger and former *New York Times* architecture critic Nicolai Ouroussoff approach a large-scale scheme and suggesting how Jacobs would have approached it differently.

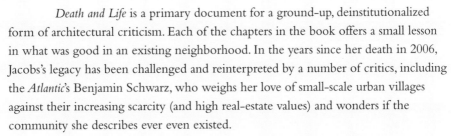

Death and Life is a primary document for a ground-up, deinstitutionalized form of architectural criticism. Each of the chapters in the book offers a small lesson in what was good in an existing neighborhood. In the years since her death in 2006, Jacobs's legacy has been challenged and reinterpreted by a number of critics, including the *Atlantic*'s Benjamin Schwarz, who weighs her love of small-scale urban villages against their increasing scarcity (and high real-estate values) and wonders if the community she describes ever even existed.

Many of the critics we have read so far have been insiders, either supported by a major publication or university, or, in the case of Olmsted, a founding member of his profession in the United States. Jacobs was not. Jacobs's book was supported by a Rockefeller Foundation grant, but the impetus for it was personal. In the early 1950s, New York City Parks Commissioner Robert Moses declared a twelve-acre area south of Washington Square Park "blighted," intending to demolish its industrial buildings and aged housing in order to build a middle-class housing project with federal Title I funds. To link this new development with Greenwich Village to the north and with his proposed Lower Manhattan Expressway to the south, Moses planned to expand the little-used carriageway that wove through the park into a four-lane road. He also intended to expand what is now LaGuardia Place into a landscaped boulevard like Park Avenue. The highway's southbound lanes would have run through the Washington Square Arch, and the fountain in the middle of the Square would have been destroyed.

Moses was not wrong when he characterized his Greenwich Village opponents, which included Jacobs, at a public hearing as "a bunch of MOTHERS!," but he failed to understand the power these mothers and other supporters could wield through the press. Images of their dissent, along with well-argued and frequent denunciations of the park-splitting plan, led to the plan's demise. Every David-and-Goliath urban tale of grassroots protesters versus big-money and/or big-government plans is now cast as a version of Jacobs versus Moses, a history well-told in Anthony Flint's 2009 book *Wrestling With Moses*.

It was during the protest over Washington Square Park that Jacobs wrote *Death and Life*. Although she harnessed the media to publicize the cause, she realized, as Flint writes, that coverage in the *New York Times* would not be enough, since the *Times* "always quoted Moses at length." Instead, she turned to the *Village Voice*, an

alternative city newspaper founded in 1955. Perhaps her most visually effective idea—one still employed whenever possible by advocates for parks and schools—was to put children front and center. The children asked for signatures, they held homemade signs, they held ribbons at a "reverse ribbon cutting" organized for news photographers. Jacobs, along with protest originator Shirley Hayes (a former actress and mother of four) and a cadre of other neighborhood women, transformed motherhood into an asset in this urban conflict. Their argument was for the values of the small versus the large, kids versus cars.

That basic argument, translated into urban terms like *parks*, *blocks*, and *border vacuums*, was embedded in Jacobs's book, which opens with a chapter (titled "The Uses of Sidewalks: Safety") on what seems like a neutral topic: "The stretch of Hudson Street where I live is each day the scene of an intricate sidewalk ballet." This is Jacobs at her most charming, describing her city in domestic, picayune detail, showing she is one of us: taking out the trash, bemused by the dietary habits of teenagers. After the high school students come the shopkeepers, opening their gates and bringing out their wares. Then the schoolchildren, the white-collar workers, and the taxis that seem to appear at just the right moment to scoop up the briefcase carriers headed down to Wall Street. This all before 9 a.m. The ballet continues through the day, a mix of commerce and socializing, the interwoven paths of longshoremen heading to bars with children on roller skates, the synchronizing of streetlights with the homecomings of all but the drinkers and night workers. Her point is not merely to make the reader desire a place in her village but to show that a neighborhood is a living, moving, working organism. All the players she describes have a role in keeping her part of the city safe, functional, and habitable: "We are the lucky possessors of a city order that makes it relatively simple to keep the peace because there are plenty of *eyes on the street* [italics added]. But there is nothing simple about that order itself, or the bewildering number of components that go into it."

This close-to-home chapter softens up the audience for Jacobs's larger argument. But by putting the reader in her shoes, she has already taken a critical *approach* distinctly different from those covered in previous chapters. She is not coming to the city (or building) cold as a disinterested observer but trying to build her argument from the ground up and the inside out. Her method of *organization* is to move from the personal, closely observed particulars to a set of unified theories (the "needs" of part two). Her approach may seem discursive, like telling a story, but the humbleness of her rhetoric should not distract from its precision. The sidewalk is the perfect starting point since it is a public space closely aligned with the private realm, and that movement from private to public is both her topic and her organizing principle.

Jacobs's account of the sidewalk ballet illustrates one way for the critic to tell the reader where he or she is coming from. Personal history informs our opinions about everything, not just architecture and urbanism. Jacobs introduces her point of origin stealthily, with an anecdote that combines the visual and the anthropological. The length and vividness of her description leads the reader to her conclusion: that every street has an order, and it is the combination of buildings and architecture that makes a city work. She manages to make her neighborhood seem like every neighborhood by itemizing its parts and describing how each one works. This makes the reader empathetic; we make the mental leap between what she says about her block, seeking a way to apply it to our own.

Few of the critics we have read so far include intimate details, but if handled properly, they have their place in the critique. Knowing that Jacobs is a downtown resident informs her book just as much as being a mother informed her Washington Square Park protest. The first case shows the kind of urban space about which she had expertise; the second, why the fight against the road was personal. It is her block that superblocks threaten; it is her children who will have to cross a large, dangerous street and be deprived of a playground. One of the hallmarks of blogging, and the move of journalism to the internet, has been the increase in first-person narrative and the deployment of anecdote. Jacobs shows how such anecdotes can be instructive, laying the groundwork for an objective argument rather than telling too much.

Jacobs, like Lewis Mumford, could also be considered a sidewalk critic: that's where her book begins, on the Hudson Street sidewalk. But while Mumford stands on the sidewalk outside Lever House and watches the crowd, Jacobs is part of that crowd. Her description of the sidewalk ballet employs the narrative techniques of the short story: showing, not telling; providing multiple characters so that any reader can find someone with whom to identify; structuring the story temporally as the scene changes from morning to night. Jacobs has an agenda, and the story has a purpose, "proving" her point that people keep cities safe, not police or security architectural elements like bollards, bomb-proof glass, or Jersey barriers.

This last is a point with particular relevance today—in a time when a bombing attempt on Times Square could be foiled by a T-shirt vendor. It was not the hardened streetscape that stopped the bomb in 2010, a security camera that recorded suspicious activity, nor a law enforcement officer that noticed something unusual, but a vendor—a commercial version of the stoop-sitters that Jacobs says will keep the peace. At the time of the bombing attempt, New York City Transportation Commissioner Janette Sadik-Khan had been remaking major intersections by turning the streets into pop-up plazas, painted sections of asphalt with tables and chairs and planters set apart for pedestrian use. These plazas were proposed as traffic-calming measures and adopted as pedestrian amenities, but they also changed the way that people moved through those intersections, adding more eyes on the street by giving people more space and by enticing them to linger. They add an extra measure of theater to crowded areas that people previously had to push through. Jacobs wrote in "The Uses of Sidewalks: Safety" about what is needed to make the streets safe in general, and her main prescriptions are foot traffic and businesses open to the sidewalk. These plazas made it natural, and good business sense, for adjacent stores to connect to the street and its new pedestrian population. She distills the lessons of the sidewalk ballet into an urban strategy, making the necessary leap from the personal to the political, Hudson Street to the city as a whole. To be effective criticism, the anecdote has to lead to a theory, the description of one block to a prescription for many.

In part two of *Death and Life*, Jacobs moves from her street to all our streets, working from her small examples to a larger point. The three points she makes about what creates a successful sidewalk are applied to the cityscape as a whole, and her *theme* develops as *diversity*. Diversity of use, diversity of users, diversity of space. What makes a successful city is diversity, what diversity produces is movement; architecture is just a frame for human activity, whether commercial or social.

If one is trying to apply Jacobs's values to urban projects today or follow in her footsteps as a critic, it is her commitment to diversity that is the most universally applicable. New urban development must learn from how the city has developed organically and build in room for difference. New critics have many opportunities to observe, describe, and classify today's successful neighborhoods in the manner of

Jacobs. Everyone can't live in Jacobs's West Village, but they can try to achieve new neighborhoods that have the same qualities of community, variety, and safety.

Jacobs identifies four conditions for generating diversity in a neighborhood or district, in her characteristic, matter-of-fact format. She makes lists. She repeats herself. Her goal is to convince as many people as possible, and to do so she sometimes resorts to the tone of the elementary-school teacher. Within her overall organizational scheme, which moves from the personal to the universal, she can be prosaic. This doesn't make for compelling rhetoric, but for someone trying to argue for a new way of looking at cities, it makes sense.

Her lists can be seen as checklists for those who might follow in her critical footsteps, signposts of what to look for in a new neighborhood. The chapters (7 through 12) in part two can be summarized as a list themselves:

1. Mixed uses. People must use the streets, sidewalks, and parks at different times and for different purposes, ensuring what we now refer to as 24/7 activity.

2. Short blocks. More corners mean more diverse real-estate options, more opportunities to change one's route, and more chances of running into people.

3. Mixed age. New real estate is expensive real estate; old buildings are better incubators for artists and entrepreneurs.

4. Concentration. The dullness of the suburbs (about which Jacobs never has anything good to say) is the result of the spreading out of people, both in space and over time. Without concentration there is no commerce, no mingling, no action. It is not difficult to imagine an updated version of *Death and Life* (or a blog) with photographs documenting the good and bad examples Jacobs describes. Her critical activities were never confined to the page, and her writing on New York maintains a link to what she experienced in three dimensions. In that spirit, the following pages of this chapter look at a three-dimensional section of New York City, one that was, like Washington Square Park, under siege by planners—this time during the early 2000s—and one that was, like Hudson Street, also a brownstone neighborhood. The project is Atlantic Yards in Brooklyn, where a basketball arena has been under construction since mid-2010. The discussion of this project shows how a contemporary critic might look at the pros and cons of the Atlantic Yards plans using Jacobs's list. It also offers examples (criticisms from two of New York City's major critics) against which to see what the Jacobs-inspired critic might write about these plans.

The Atlantic Yards project, the $4.2 billion, twenty-one-acre mixed-use project unveiled in December 2003, was to be developed by Forest City Ratner, designed by Frank Gehry, and built partly on a new deck over the Metropolitan Transportation Authority's Vanderbilt rail yard in Brooklyn. The project sits between two largely row-house neighborhoods, Prospect Heights and Fort Greene, and over a major transportation hub linking the New York City subway to the Long Island commuter rail. The initial versions of the plan included 2,250 affordable rental apartments (along with 4,610 market-rate rentals and condominiums), 4.5 million square feet of office space, and a hotel in sixteen towers ranging from nineteen to fifty-eight stories, along with—and this was its initial selling point—a nineteen-thousand-seat professional basketball arena for what would become the National Basketball Association's Brooklyn Nets. Gehry's initial design proposal cleverly embedded this arena in a ring of architecturally ambitious buildings, some clad in rippling metal, some blocky, colorful and childlike. The tallest, at the intersection of Flatbush and Atlantic avenues, was a diaphanous tower christened Miss Brooklyn. At 620 feet, Miss Brooklyn would have been Brooklyn's tallest building.

On the blocks south of this major intersection, Gehry proposed an array of residential towers to be placed adjacent to the existing residential neighborhoods, and following the street grid of Prospect Heights. These towers, much taller than the three- and four-story brownstones, were arranged around the edges of a new superblock made by eliminating cross streets and enclosed an irregularly shaped open space designated as a public park. The most expensive part of the project was a deck that would span the open rail yard, bridging the tracks and thereby creating new, buildable area. The project also claimed several blocks currently occupied by a mixture of residential and industrial buildings. If the residents and owners of those buildings did not vacate, Forest City Ratner would invoke eminent domain by arguing—as Moses had of Washington Square South—that the area was "blighted." A block of Pacific Street, which these buildings fronted, was to be demapped (removed as a city street) in order to accommodate the circumference of the arena.

Ouroussoff, in a review titled "Seeking First to Reinvent the Sports Arena, and Then Brooklyn" that appeared in the *New York Times* on July 5, 2005, had nothing but praise for the architecture:

> If [Frank Gehry's new design] is approved, it will radically alter the
> Brooklyn skyline, reaffirming the borough's emergence as a legitimate
> cultural rival to Manhattan....
>
> There are those—especially acolytes of the urbanist Jane
> Jacobs—who will complain about the development's humongous size.
> But cities attain their beauty from their mix of scales; one could see the
> development's thrusting forms as a representation of Brooklyn's cultural
> flowering.

For Ouroussoff the neighborhood's promise was all in the future. Gehry's design would prove that arenas did not have to be urban wastelands (like the area around Madison Square Garden in Manhattan) and new residential developments did not need to be cloaked in neohistorical detailing (like Battery Park City in Manhattan). The fact that Gehry was interested in designing something for Brooklyn was a sign the borough had arrived, and the flowing forms of Miss Brooklyn would become a sort of architectural trophy. Ouroussoff, not typically an emotional writer, is roused here to deploy a panoply of superlatives ("most important urban development plan...in decades" is a version of the over-the-top historical comparisons used by critics in skyscraper reviews) and active adjectives (clashing, undulating, cascading, also skyscraper language). His language reveals what he may not have recognized himself: he was reviewing this urban plan like a skyscraper, dazzled by its newness and its nextness, and treating it as a sculpture to be deposited on a tabula rasa. At only one point in the review does he touch down into Brooklyn. Everything else is about the model and plans, Gehry and his career, and the history of arena and large-scale planning. His theme is that Gehry saves the city, and his approach is to describe the Atlantic Yards proposal as something that has already happened. He dismisses critics as stuck in a sentimental, Jacobsian idea of the successful neighborhood as, by nature, low-rise, and argues that Gehry has taken care of any scale problems by stepping the towers down, from the center of the block to the sidewalk edge, to meet the height of the existing brownstones: "What is more, Mr. Gehry has gone to great lengths to fuse his design with its surroundings. The tallest of the towers, for example, are mostly set along Atlantic Avenue, where they face a mix of retail malls and low-income housing. Along Dean Street, the buildings' low, stocky forms are more in keeping with the rows of brownstones that extend south into Park Slope." Whether or not this gesture would have been enough to "fuse" Gehry and nineteenth-century brownstones is a matter of opinion. But it is clear from Ouroussoff's overall approach that his focus is elsewhere than Brooklyn.

For a critic inspired by Jacobs, Dean Street is precisely where the review would begin, on the sidewalks. Where is the ballet? One would observe the nature of the neighborhood as it exists and consider the questions of "blight," safety, diversity, block size, and building age Jacobs asked of her own neighborhood and of New York in the 1960s. In the Atlantic Yards development footprint, there are two different dances happening. The first occurs close to the busy intersection of Flatbush and Atlantic avenues, opposite the site of the future arena. There, two malls developed by Forest City Ratner in the 1990s and early 2000s occupy two blocks of Atlantic Avenue. Both are successful financially and failures architecturally—boxy, unengaging, with unpleasantly hot interior hallways and no central atrium. More importantly for a critic following Jacobs, neither has shops that open onto the street. Pedestrians hurry swiftly past the primarily blank, block-long walls of both malls, looking for the entrance doors.

In chapter 9, "The Need for Small Blocks," Jacobs describes what large buildings without doors onto the street do to cities: "They automatically sort people into paths that meet too infrequently, so that different uses near each other geographically are, in practical effect, literally blocked off from one another." So it is with the malls. To get from one to the other, to get from one store to another, is a disorienting and unpleasant experience. There is no possibility for window shopping. This sorting creates what Jacobs calls a "border vacuum," a no-man's-land that is unsafe (no eyes on the street) and often an eyesore (no sense of ownership). And the new development plan would have more of the same on the opposite side of the street. Along the long Atlantic Avenue side of the arena, Gehry attempted to offset the ill effects of these by cutting windows into the ground floor. Pedestrians would be able to see the basketball patrons inside, and the lights of the arena would have brightened the sidewalk, but there would still have been little reason for people to walk these blocks.

Having examined the situation on the avenues and having found a lack of pedestrian diversity, density, and accessibility, the Jacobsian critic would then move to the smaller streets of the Prospect Heights neighborhood. In chapter 9 Jacobs also argues that such blocks offer more possible routes through a given section of the city, which would bring a diversity of businesses and users. Smaller blocks would also mean more corner buildings (which make more attractive storefronts); stores attract users who may not live in the immediate vicinity. Variety prevents residential torpor. In "Visual Order: Its Limits and Possibilities," chapter 19 in part four of *Death and Life*, Jacobs makes the point that streets work better when they do not seem homogenous; without stores, planting, and parks to make routes interesting, "these paths are meaningless because all their scenes are essentially the same." The dance she describes on Hudson Street is a dance of diversity, and that was the dance on Dean and Pacific streets in 2005.

Prospect Heights is crisscrossed with just the kind of small streets Jacobs prefers, with houses in the center of the blocks, businesses at the corners, and retail corridors on the larger avenues. Side streets feature artists studios and repair shops, where row houses were replaced long ago with industrial buildings and garages. These mixed uses bring life to the streets when most of its residents are at work. After dark the lit-up lobbies of the new condominiums (on the long blocks of Pacific and Dean streets) in renovated old buildings and the traffic of residents to them increase safety, as did the late hours of Freddy's Bar (now moved elsewhere). The Jacobsian critic would notice that the buildings are of mixed ages, ranging from tenements of the nineteenth century to new construction and renovation of the late twentieth, which makes for the vibrant neighborhoods Jacobs describes in chapter 10, "The Need for Aged Buildings." Where was the blight?

The Atlantic Yards plan as initially proposed did promise a number of neo-Jacobsian elements. The buildings were to include a basketball arena, white-collar office space, retail stores, and residential apartments (a mix of rentals and condominiums, with 30 percent of rentals offered at below-market rates)—mixed-use and mixed-income, if not mixed in age or in design. The arena's ground floor was to have eyes on the street. The stepped heights of the residential towers nodded to the existing neighborhood fabric. But even critics sympathetic to Gehry, like Goldberger, suggested it might be better for a new neighborhood to be designed more than a single architect. Even if all of the architecture is built at once, it could still come from a variety of hands, like in a real city. In "Gehry-Rigged" (2006) Goldberger writes,

> Yet Gehry's design is a large part of the problem. He told me that he accepted the job in part because he has never taken on this kind of urban challenge, but his talents hardly seem suited to it. Gehry's great success has come from architectural jewels that sparkle against the background of the rest of a city. . . . In Brooklyn, the task is to create a coherent cityscape that relates comfortably to its surroundings. Gehry tried to do this by grouping some understated towers around a few very elaborate ones. . . . Rather than giving a sense of foreground and background, the juxtaposition of plain and fancy just looks like a few Gehrys bought for full price next to several bought at discount.

Goldberger is sympathetic to Gehry, as he is to most of the architects about whom he writes. Both he and Ouroussoff see the Atlantic Yards development as primarily an opportunity for Gehry to show his skills as an urban planner as well as an architect. Neither focuses on the city as it exists, preferring to dwell on the imagined Brooklyn. When contrasted with the ground-up criticism of Jacobs, one can see the emperor's-new-clothes aspect of this critical approach. Why are they treating Brooklyn as "background"? What is already there that Gehry is replacing? Who decided that affirmation of the borough's "cultural flowering" was necessary? The difference a critical approach can make is put into stark relief in these examples of urban criticism, where there is so much the writer leaves out.

On March 11, 2010, ground was broken for an arena at the corner of Atlantic and Flatbush avenues. But not Gehry's arena. After years of denials and a slow scaling back of the project's urban goals, Gehry was no longer involved. Urban development that was to remake Brooklyn's skyline began instead with the construction of a what is now known as the Barclays Center, designed by SHoP Architects and Ellerbe Beckett. The rest of the buildings, architects unknown, may be built in the future. New York City real-estate blogs, which had chronicled the five-year drama, followed the emotional arc of some Brooklyn residents from elation

at the first renderings to disappointment at the public process, anger at the bait-and-switch of architects, and resignation when the next-to-last lawsuit from those who lived in the footprint was lost. Jacobs's legacy was evident in the idea of a written protest, that citizens had a voice in making (or unmaking) their cities and that the small changes underway in a neighborhood before the starchitects came calling could be as transformative as the large, clashing, undulating, cascading intervention.

There are entire books devoted to different interpretations of Jacobs's legacy for the planning of cities. In this book her legacy comes from the connection between her account of the sidewalk ballet on Hudson Street and her list of urban "needs." It is essential that the critic read other critics' works to understand history and rhetoric, to show authority and discuss his or her thought process. But above all, the critic needs to walk.

In the introduction, Ada Louise Huxtable writes about walking around a single building, Marine Midland, and turns that walk into a meditation on the shape of public space, the face of corporate architecture, and the history of downtown Manhattan development. In this chapter, Jacobs turns a stroll down her block into a book-length dissertation on diversity of space, of age, of use as urban necessities. Both critics emphasize the facts on the ground rather than the cities in the air, what people are doing rather than what architects want to do. There's a suitable parallelism between the approaches of these two women and a stark contrast with the criticisms of the skyscraper (all male) in chapter one. Cities are not towers, and should not be critiqued as such.

CHECKLIST

1. Identify a large urban development project in your city. Walk the existing site and make note of what and who is there. Apply Jacobs's lists to the area: Does it have mixed uses? Mixed-age buildings? Long or short blocks? Eyes on the street? Who uses the streets and parks? At what times of day?

2. Ask the same questions of the proposed development project, working from public plans and renderings. Does the new plan have Jacobsian elements?

3. Read the news about the project and start tracking its progress. Begin writing when you can identify an urban perspective that isn't being voiced by other critics and journalists. Introduce the element of time into your writing, in blog form (for more information on blogging, see pages 176–79), with short posts (no more than five hundred words) commenting on what you see, read, and hear. Try to write at least once a week, following the project over a period of months.

4. Think about how using the blog form for criticism informs your outlook on the project and your writing. Does your opinion change? Do your loyalties shift? How do time and familiarity impact your critique?

More Than One Way to Skin a Building

AT THE CORE OF JANE JACOBS'S WRITING about the city is the idea of diversity: varied ages of buildings and of their users, different times of day and quantities of sunlight, multiple uses and shapes of space. The same is true of writing about architecture. There is no single best way, just as there is no one best skyscraper (no matter what architects claim). In this book I have shown the diversity within the critical field and suggested ways each of the critics quoted can inform contemporary criticism of architectural types.

The architecture review has a basic form, one that is still valid despite changes in publishing—especially the parameters brought on by digital publishing. But within and beyond the template of *theme*, *approach*, and *organization*, description, argument, and conclusions vary. Writing style is personal, developed over time and with practice. And one's approach to a building is also personal. There is no shame in reviving a theme, analyzing the organization, or taking inspiration from the approach of previous critics. Following in their footsteps, literally and figuratively, is how we learn. Each building or urban plan is a new opportunity to haul out the superlatives, kick the foundation, and learn from experience how it works.

The questions I have asked you to consider here have been developed over five years of teaching. As I mentioned in the introduction, I always take the class to review one building. Sometimes the resulting papers read as if everyone had written their reviews in the same room, offering simultaneous thumbs up and thumbs down to each feature—from facade to lobby, gallery to seating. More often what comes back makes me see the space anew, toggling between the vision of one student and another as if given ten to fifteen new sets of eyes. Love, hate, indifference. A history of the type or a feminist critique of the bathrooms. We all walk down the same streets, but what we see is filtered through the lenses of experience, politics, aesthetics, and emotion. Digital publishing has made it easier to select one of those views and to send that perspective out into the world.

The writers discussed in this book are of foundational importance for the field of architecture criticism. The pieces reprinted have structure, sustained argument, and carefully considered sentences that offer a sense that the authors know exactly where the end is. But the future of architecture criticism may not lie with their approach, as the field is currently going in a number of different directions. The best-known blogs on architecture—like *BLDGBLOG*, *City of Sound*, *A Daily Dose of Architecture*, *Mammoth*, *Strange Harvest*, to name a few—have arguments sustained over days, weeks, years. To excerpt them is to place too much scrutiny on a single piece of writing that was typically intended as a continuing rant or conversation—and didn't make sense in an analog book. The theme that individual blogs and bloggers pursue is not always apparent in a single post, and the approach of a blog is clear only if you have been following along from the beginning. The organization of the individual post, as on most blogs, is linear: statement, exegesis, abrupt end.

The work of many of the critics discussed in this book is available online and a number of them (Blair Kamin, Karrie Jacobs, Paul Goldberger) do blog, but their online work is different in tone from their formal columns. The difference between what is written for publication and what is blogged is often a matter of dimension: the blog, by virtue of its frequency, usually has to be about architecture seen in rendering or through photographs, or described in other people's writing. Few have the time, money, and energy to blog about architecture and urbanism seen in three dimensions every (or every other) day. The architecture critic of today has to blog, but it is a discipline best learned through practice. (Go to WordPress or Tumblr. Pick a template. Start blogging.) The effect of the internet on architecture criticism has largely been on the means of delivery rather than the form. The review is still the review. The blog is something else, and its effect on architecture and criticism still to be determined.

That said, the internet is a wonderful place to find communities of criticism, the data required to fuel that criticism, and a megaphone to broadcast criticism. When Jacobs and her colleagues found that the *New York Times* was not giving them equal time, they went to the *Village Voice*, a forum willing and able to amplify their dissent, visually and verbally, making David as large as Goliath in rhetorical terms. If Jacobs's deeds are as important as her written words, her legacy can be seen in the way protests about top-down planning for public space are organized on the internet and by media-savvy city dwellers. Dissent over the use of eminent domain or the demolition of historic structures (organized via Facebook, distributed by Twitter, and given voice by determined bloggers) all reveal the activist spirit of Jacobs. If Jacobs were alive today she, or her supporters, would be blogging, tweeting, and sending daily press releases to popular real-estate websites like *Curbed*.

I mention *Curbed* because it functions in New York and the six other cities in which it operates much as the *Village Voice* did for Jacobs: as an alternative press, broadcasting small voices (as long as they are newsworthy) as loudly and frequently as the booming voice of the mainstream press. *Brownstoner*, a Brooklyn-specific blog, is an even better analogue to what the *Voice* was in the 1960s, as it has developed from a renovation blog to a clearing-house for brownstone Brooklyn news, boosterism, and community organizing. Neither offers architecture criticism per se but instead the fodder for it, asking questions the critic should answer, showing sites the critic should visit, and poking fun at critics who fail to keep their cool.

Brownstoner was created in 2004 by Jonathan Butler, a frustrated Wall Street broker who had recently purchased a run-down brownstone in Clinton Hill in Brooklyn. *Curbed*, founded in 2004 by Lockhart Steele, was a site also born of one man's interest in the changing city, but one that quickly grew to focus on real estate in all its stages, from development proposals, renderings, and images of construction sites to sales information, price reductions, and, finally, habitation. Steele's obsession with the changing face of the city during an unprecedented building boom turned out to be one shared by millions. The tone on *Curbed* is snarky; *Brownstoner*, earnest. If the *New York Times* was not representing the opposition to Atlantic Yards thoroughly (and it couldn't, because Forest City Ratner was the paper's development partner for their new Midtown building under construction at the time), protest groups could go to blogs. Only on *Curbed* and *Brownstoner* could the whole story be told—press release by press release, lawsuit by lawsuit—because only online was there the time and the space to cover the real complexity of making urban architecture.

The Atlantic Yards opposition illustrates the effectiveness of the blog for activist critique. The opposition organized online, choosing a name that clearly stated their position: Develop Don't Destroy Brooklyn (DDDB). DDDB signed up influential Brooklyn residents as supporters, including authors, actors, editors, and architects, and allied itself with younger politicians in the borough. Jonathan Lethem, an award-winning author and member of the DDDB board, wrote a dissent, "Brooklyn's Trojan Horse," on *Slate*. Less famous supporters set up their own blogs, creating a swarm of alternative, focused sources of information and critique. *Atlantic Yards Report* set itself the task of fact-checking first the *Times* coverage of the project, then all media coverage and press releases, offering the kind of follow-up rarely found in physical papers. *Brooklyn Views*, an architect's blog, created renderings of the size and shape of the proposed buildings without Gehry's styling and superimposed them on photographs of the streets under the headline, "It's the Scale, Stupid." *Noticing New York*, a blog by real-estate attorney and planner Michael D. D. White, even started the Jane Jacobs Atlantic Yards Report Card, based on forty-seven criteria he says Jacobs uses in *Death and Life*.

For the critic, all of these blogs offer a lesson in sustainability: picking a topic and sticking to it, maintaining a consistent tone, becoming the place to go for a specific kind of critique. Bloggers can become architecture critics for a cause, slicing off one piece of the city to analyze and critique because the infinite space of the internet allows for that expansion. They can also become architecture critics for a theme (*BLDGBLOG* is a great example of this, claiming as its field "architectural conjecture, urban speculation, and landscape futures," and finding architecture everywhere but where well-known architects have placed it), clearing houses for a specific kind of architectural information that is international, digital, sometime fictional, but drawn together by an individual's sensibility and writing. Almost all the MFA students in the School of Visual Arts D-Crit program have their own blogs, from minimal Tumblrs with links to images of interest to professional platforms that showcase all of their writing. Blogging is, in fact, a course requirement.

As I was completing this manuscript, D-Crit published the work of its 2010 graduates in a small chapbook titled *At Water's Edge*. The topic is the New York City shoreline, covered in ten short essays. The students' approaches were all over the map: a personal history of growing up on an island near Niagara Falls, my-first-trip-to-Queens astonishment, a poetic meditation on the word *beyond*, and an account of the scruffy decor and cigarette smoke of Water Taxi Beach in Long Island City. Their essays could have served as alternate examples for the chapters of this book, as the waterfront encompasses skyscrapers, museums, parks, and failing urban ideas. Their themes come across in wonderfully evocative opening paragraphs, showing an economy of means and access to the kind of descriptive, personal writing that allows the reader to identify with the critics, whether or not they ultimately agree.

What the pieces have in common is close observation, attention to language, and an overriding sense of place. If *Writing About Architecture* teaches you anything, it should be to pay close attention to wherever you are. In "Sometimes We Get It Right," Huxtable stands on one New York City corner, reading across the facades of different eras, editing the sights into a coherent argument, discarding the pieces that don't fit. Jacobs hangs out her window, watching the people on her street with the same intensity, editing their jerky diurnal movements into another sort of coherent argument—a ballet. The profession of architecture critic is a small one, and not one scheduled for growth, but the ability to write about architecture—either as a language or as a stage—is relevant to more than criticism. Architecture is the art you cannot avoid and one that critics can't make go away. My hope is that after reading this book and trying to answer the questions posed, you won't want it to go away. You'll try to make it better.

ACKNOWLEDGMENTS

Mosette Broderick, director of the Urban Design and Architecture Studies program at New York University, is the person without whom this book could not have been written. It was she who asked me to teach a senior seminar. When I asked her what I should teach, she replied, "Architecture criticism!," as if it went without saying. Her encouragement, and continuing employment, created the course that led to this book. Much credit also goes to Alice Twemlow, cofounder of the MFA Design Criticism department at the School of Visual Arts, for adopting my class and introducing me to the wonders of graduate teaching.

I am grateful to the authors, publishers, and estates that allowed me to reprint the work of these amazing critics: Gina Maccoby of the Gina Maccoby Literary Agency; Michael Sorkin; Steve Weingarten and the estate of Charles W. Moore; the Frederick Law Olmsted Papers, Manuscript Division, Library of Congress; the New York Times; and Random House, Inc.

Thank you to my writing and architecture teachers: Alan Plattus, Alec Purves, Fred Strebeigh, and Vincent Scully at Yale; Jean-Louis Cohen at the Institute of Fine Arts; Barry Bergdoll and Joan Ockman at Columbia.

Thank you to my brother, Jeremy M. Lange, for taking on a new challenge, and making our childhood artistic coproductions an adult reality.

Thank you to Princeton Architectural Press for taking on this project: to Clare Jacobson for her original interest in my proposal, and to my editor, Linda Lee, for seeing it through the transformation to publication. Deb Wood gave the book a design identity as rigorous and playful as the critics covered in its two-tone pages.

And finally, my sincere appreciation to all the students who have taken my course. Without your hard work and perseverance, I would not have learned how to teach and would not know nearly as much about how to write.

IMAGE KEY

INTRODUCTION

CH. 1

CH. 2

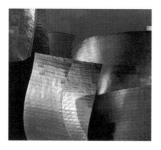

PAGE 44:
Frank O. Gehry,
Guggenheim Museum
Bilbao, 1997

PAGES 58–67:
Frank Lloyd Wright,
Solomon R. Guggenheim
Museum, 1959

PAGES 68–69:
Frank Lloyd Wright,
Solomon R. Guggenheim
Museum, 1959

PAGE 70:
Marcel Breuer & Associates,
Whitney Museum of American
Art, 1966

PAGES 77–87:
Albert C. Ledner & Associates,
O'Toole Medical Services Building,
1964

CH. 3

PAGES 88–89:
Albert C. Ledner & Associates,
O'Toole Medical Services Building,
1964

PAGES 90–91:
Marcel Breuer & Associates,
Whitney Museum of American
Art, 1966

CH. 4

PAGE 92:
Pier 17, South Street Seaport,
Franklin D. Roosevelt East River
Drive in the background

PAGE 104–15:
Morphosis Architects,
41 Cooper Square, 2009

PAGE 116–19:
Morphosis Architects,
41 Cooper Square, 2009

CH. 5

PAGE 120:
Frederick Law Olmsted and
Calvert Vaux, Central Park,
1858–76

PAGES 134–45:
James Corner Field Operations and
Diller Scofidio + Renfro, The High
Line, section 1, 2009

CH. 6

PAGE 146:
Washington Square Park
Fountain, reconstructed
2009

PAGES 159–63:
Brownstone Brooklyn

PAGES 164–67:
Stanford White,
Washington Arch, 1895

PAGES 168–73:
Future site of the
Barclays Center,
Brooklyn, 2010

SOURCES

INTRODUCTION

Adams, Nicholas. *Skidmore, Owings & Merrill: SOM since 1936*. London: Phaidon, 2007.

Huxtable, Ada Louise. *Kicked a Building Lately*? New York: Quadrangle/The New York Times Book Co., 1976.

———. *On Architecture: Collected Reflections on a Century of Change*. New York: Walker & Company, 2008.

———. "Sometimes We Do It Right." In *Will They Ever Finish Bruckner Boulevard?* New York: Macmillan Company, 1970. Originally published in the *New York Times*, March 31, 1968.

Stern, Robert A. M., Thomas Mellins, and David Fishman. *New York 1960: Architecture and Urbanism between the Second World War and the Bicentennial*. New York: Monacelli Press, 1995.

White, Norval, and Elliot Willensky. *AIA Guide to New York City*. 4th ed. New York: Three Rivers Press, 2000.

CH.1

Adams, Nicholas. *Skidmore, Owings & Merrill: S.O.M. since 1936*. London: Phaidon, 2007.

Goldberger, Paul. "Triangulation." In *Building Up and Tearing Down*, 148–51. New York: Monacelli Press, 2009. Originally published in the *New Yorker*, December 19, 2005.

Huxtable, Ada Louise. "The Park Avenue School of Architecture." *New York Times Magazine*. December 15, 1957, 30–31, 54–56.

Mumford, Lewis. "House of Glass." In *From the Ground Up: Observations on Contemporary Architecture, Housing, Highway Building, and Civic Design*, 156–66. New York: Harcourt, Brace and Company, 1956. Originally published as "The Sky Line: House of Glass" in the *New Yorker*, August 9, 1952.

———. *Sidewalk Critic: Lewis Mumford's Writings on New York*. Edited by Robert Wojtowicz. New York: Princeton Architectural Press, 1998.

Stern, Robert A. M., David Fishman, and Jacob Tilove. *New York 2000: Architecture and Urbanism from the Bicentennial to the Millennium*. New York: The Monacelli Press, 2006.

Sullivan, Louis. "The Tall Office Building Artistically Considered." In *America Builds: Source Documents in American Architecture and Planning*, 340–46. Edited by Leland M. Roth. New York: Harper & Row, 1983. Originally published in *Lippincott's Magazine*, March 1896.

CH.2

Florida, Richard. *The Rise of the Creative Class: And How It's Transforming Work, Leisure, Community and Everyday Life*. New York: Basic Books, 2002.

Huxtable, Ada Louise. "The Guggenheim Bilbao: Art and Architecture as One." In *On Architecture: Collected Reflections on a Century of Change*, 107–11. New York: Walker & Company, 2008. Originally published in the *Wall Street Journal*, October 16, 1997.

———. "What Should A Museum Be?" In *On Architecture*, 93–99. Originally published in the *New York Times*, May 8, 1960.

Muschamp, Herbert. "The Miracle in Bilbao." In *Hearts of the City: The Selected Writings of Herbert Muschamp*, 424–35. New York: Random House, 2009. Originally published in the *New York Times Magazine*, September 7, 1997.

———. "A Queens Factory Is Born Again, as a Church." *The New York Times*, September 5, 1999.

———. "Trump, His Gilded Taste, and Me." In *Hearts of the City*, 539–50. Originally published in the *New York Times*, December 19, 1999.

Newhouse, Victoria. *Towards a New Museum*. Expanded ed. New York: Monacelli Press, 2006.

Rybcinski, Witold. "The Bilbao Effect." *The Atlantic*, September 2002.

CH.3

Davidson, Justin. "St. Anywhere." *New York*, March 23, 2009, 10.

Huxtable, Ada Louise, "Lively Original Versus Dead Copy." In *Will They Ever Finish Bruckner Boulevard?*, 211–12. Berkeley: University of California Press, 1970. Originally published in the *New York Times*, May 9, 1965.

Kamin, Blair. *Why Architecture Matters: Lessons from Chicago*. Chicago: University of Chicago Press, 2001.

Riegl, Alois. "The Modern Cult of Monuments: Its Character and Its Origin," reprinted in *Oppositions* 25 (Fall 1982): 21–51. Originally published as *Der moderne Denkmalkultus: Sein Wesen und seine Entstehung* (Vienna: W. Braumuller, 1903).

Sorkin, Michael. "Save the Whitney." In *Exquisite Corpse: Writing on Buildings*, 119–24. New York: Verso, 1991. Originally published in the *Village Voice,* June 25, 1985.

CH.4

Banham, Reyner. *Los Angeles: The Architecture of Four Ecologies*. Berkeley and Los Angeles: University of California Press, 2009. Originally published by Harper & Row, 1971.

Davis, Mike. "Fortress L.A." In *City of Quartz: Excavating the Future in Los Angeles*, 221–63. New York: Verso, 1990.

Moore, Charles W. "You Have to Pay for the Public Life." In Y*ou Have to Pay for the Public Life: Selected Essays of Charles W. Moore*, 111–41. Edited by Kevin Keim. Cambridge, MA: MIT Press, 2001. Originally published in *Perspecta 9/10* (1965).

Sorkin, Michael. "Finding an Open Space for the Exercise of Democracy in New York's Dense Urban Fabric." *Architectural Record*, October 2004, 85–87.

Venturi, Robert. *Complexity and Contradiction in Architecture*. New York: Museum of Modern Art, 1966. Originally published in *Perspecta 9/10* (1965).

Venturi, Robert, Steven Izenour, and Denise Scott Brown. *Learning from Las Vegas.* Cambridge, MA: MIT Press, 1972.

Whyte, William H. *The Social Life of Small Urban Spaces*. New York: Project for Public Spaces, 2001. Originally published by the Conservation Society, 1980.

CH.5

Huxtable, Ada Louise. "Down-to-Earth Masterpieces of Public Landscape Design." *The Wall Street Journal*, May 4, 2005, D10.

Jacobs, Karrie. "America: Beyond the Hype." *Metropolis*, June 2009, 58, 60, 62.

Olmsted, Frederick Law. *Civilizing American Cities: A Selection of Frederick Law Olmsted's Writings on City Landscapes*. Edited by S. B. Sutton. Cambridge, MA: MIT Press, 1971.

———. "Public Parks and the Enlargement of Towns." In *America Builds: Source Documents in American Architecture and Planning,* 182–91. Edited by Leland M. Roth. New York: Harper & Row, 1983.

Reed, Peter Shedd. *Groundswell: Constructing the Contemporary Landscape.* New York: Museum of Modern Art, 2005.

Rogers, Elizabeth Barlow. *Landscape Design: A Cultural and Architectural History.* New York: Harry N. Abrams, 2001.

Rybczynski, Witold. *A Clearing in the Distance: Frederick Law Olmsted and America in the Nineteenth Century.* New York: Scribner, 1999.

Wharton, Edith. *The Age of Innocence.* New York: Modern Library, 1999. Originally published *Pictorial Review* magazine, July—October, 1920.

CH.6

Ballon, Hilary, and Kenneth T. Jackson, eds. *Robert Moses and the Modern City: The Transformation of New York.* New York: W. W. Norton, 2007.

Carr, Cynthia. "Life in the Footprint." *Village Voice*, August 2–August 8, 2006, 27–30.

Flint, Anthony. *Wrestling with Moses: How Jane Jacobs Took on New York's Master Builder and Transformed the American City.* New York: Random House, 2009.

Goldberger, Paul. "Gehry-Rigged." In *Building Up and Tearing Down*, 160–63. New York: Monacelli Press, 2009. Originally published in the *New Yorker*, October 16, 2006.

Lange, Alexandra. "New Improved Brooklyn." *New York*, May 3, 2004, 28–35, 105–6.

Jacobs, Jane. *The Death and Life of Great American Cities.* New York: Random House, 1961.

Ouroussoff, Nicolai. "Seeking First to Reinvent the Sports Arena, and Then Brooklyn." *New York Times*, July 5, 2005.

Schwarz, Benjamin. "Gentrification and Its Discontents." *The Atlantic Monthly*, June 2010, 85–88.

Smith, Chris. "Mr. Ratner's Neighborhood." *New York*, August 14, 2006, 24–32.

CONCLUSION

Busch, Akiko, Saundra Marcel, and Vera Sacchetti, eds. *At Water's Edge*. New York: School of Visual Arts, 2011.

Lethem, Jonathan. "Brooklyn's Trojan Horse." *Slate*, June 19, 2006. http://www .slate.com/id/2143634/.